UNIVERSITY OF
GLOUCESTERSHIRE

WALES IN THE 21st CENTURY

Wales in the 21st Century

An Economic Future

Edited by

Jane Bryan
and
Calvin Jones

Foreword by Garel Rhys

MACMILLAN
Business

First published in Great Britain 2000 by
MACMILLAN PRESS LTD
Houndmills, Basingstoke, Hampshire RG21 6XS and London
Companies and representatives throughout the world

A catalogue record for this book is available from the British Library.

ISBN 0–333–79373–0

 First published in the United States of America 2000 by
ST. MARTIN'S PRESS, INC.,
Scholarly and Reference Division,
175 Fifth Avenue, New York, N.Y. 10010

ISBN 0–312–23306–X

Library of Congress Cataloging-in-Publication Data

Wales in the twenty-first century / edited by Jane Bryan and Calvin Jones.
p.   cm.
Includes bibliographical references and index.
ISBN 0—312–23306–X
1. Wales—Civilization. 2. Wales—Forecasting. I. Title: Wales in the 21st century. II. Bryan, Jane, 1956– III. Jones, Calvin, 1969–

DA711.5.W345 2000
942.9—dc21

00–020452

Selection and editorial matter © Jane Bryan and Calvin Jones 2000
Foreword © Garel Rhys 2000
Individual chapters (in order) © Stephen Hill, Calvin Jones, Karl Taylor and Jane Bryan,
Max Munday, Jane Bryan, Gillian Bristow, Jane Bryan, David Brooksbank and David
Pickernell, Meirion Thomas and Martin Rhisiart, Annette Roberts, Stephen Hill 2000

This book is printed on paper suitable for recycling and made from fully managed and
sustained forest sources.

10   9   8   7   6   5   4   3   2   1
09   08   07   06   05   04   03   02   01   00

Printed in Great Britain
by Antony Rowe Ltd., Chippenham, Wiltshire.

Contents

List of Tables and Figures

Tables

Figures

Foreword

While too few books singularly attend to Welsh issues, those that do have to answer several challenges, and particularly so as Wales enters a new era of self-governance and, indeed, a new century. Entering the third millennium is only notionally a new beginning but with so much rapid change in both the political and economic arena, and the prospect of greater enlightenment and expectation among the Welsh people, the new century is a fitting springboard for a work which draws together the past, present and future as its purpose.

Wales today is a product of its past, and Wales of the future is already being shaped by how we understand the present. Nineteenth-century Wales was essentially a village economy, transformed by dense clusters of coal and steel activity, sitting alongside the old agrarian tradition. There followed a further wave of restructuring with the introduction of more diversified manufacturing, much of it inward investment from the rest of UK and elsewhere, which widened the old narrow base and contributed to the growth of cities and towns, joined by new infrastructure. Towards the end of the twentieth century a new shift from manufacturing to the service industry, in common with the rest of the developed world, is beginning to prevail, requiring still more adjustment by the Welsh people.

Many of the more recent changes have been managed, through regional policy tools, by the Welsh Office and the development agencies, not only to mitigate high unemployment but also to pursue a prosperity goal that will ensure that the Welsh people are at least as well off as the rest of the United Kingdom. Sadly, in this regard, the most cogent lesson of the last years of the last century is that Wales has not yet caught up and, indeed, has to fight hard merely to stand still, despite its success in attracting foreign investment and the energetic efforts of policy executives.

The first challenge to be met by this book is fixing the present into the past. Chapter 1 provides an introductory background followed by Chapters 2 and 3 which look at the roots of disadvantage faced by Wales in terms of industrial and occupational structure and incomes, demonstrating that understanding the past is critical to adjusting the future.

Of course, this book is about the future, so the second challenge is to fix that future into the present, principally by deepening our understanding of policy direction and its outcomes. Chapter 4 addresses the complex, and perhaps vexatious, nature of foreign direct investment, which has been central to policy efforts designed to relieve high unemployment in Wales over the past sixty or so years. This chapter asks serious questions about its limitations and points to possible routes to optimising past and future initiatives. Chapter 5 calls for a new pragmatism regarding policy for small firms and offers, in a sense, an antidote, tempered by realism, to investment from without. Nor is agriculture neglected, despite its vastly changed configuration, and this is given a thorough and authoritative review in Chapter 6.

Chapter 7 considers the implications of modern international transport thinking on how infrastructure will be used in the future, and provokes the reader to consider the role of individuals and firms in attaining sustainable movement from place to place. Chapter 8 focuses on the time-limited opportunity to use Objective 1 status and takes the Valleys region as an exemplar for a range of policy objectives. Chapter 9 considers the role of innovation in transforming Wales, while the two final chapters review policy targets, suggest the direction future exploration should take, and draw together some concluding arguments.

The next challenge is to the readers of this volume, rather than its authors who have, I think, discharged their duty in its preparation. The challenge for the readers, who will probably be familiar with Wales and its problems, is to be responsive to the many stimuli contained within; to question the ideas expressed, to perhaps concur, or if they find themselves in disagreement to frame constructive ripostes and alternatives.

The ultimate challenge belongs to all of us, in Wales. Rejecting the words of Dylan Thomas, '*The land of my fathers. My fathers can have it*', Wales of the future belongs to its sons and daughters who will, one day soon, have much to be proud of. Already one senses a new self-confidence in the young of Wales.

Finally, one criticism of academics is that their 'ivory tower' perspective is too divorced from reality to have any value in the 'substantive world'. However, that 'tower' yields some benefit. It can provide an objective panorama, freed from the strait-jacket of framing goals according to what can be achieved in one term of office, be it in national government, the Assembly or a local authority, and untainted by political correctness. Hence, many of the observations in this book may lack comfort for the reader but then '*all rising to great place is by a winding stair*' (Francis Bacon, 1561–1626).

GAREL RHYS
Professor of Economics
Cardiff Business School

Notes on the Contributors

Gillian Bristow is a Research Associate at the Cardiff Business School. Her research interests include integrated rural development, EU agricultural policy and the Structural Funds.

David Brooksbank is assistant head of the Welsh Enterprise Institute as well as a Principal Lecturer in Economics at the University of Glamorgan Business School.

Jane Bryan is a Research Associate in the Welsh Economy Research Unit. Her research interests include the performance of small manufacturing firms, regional infrastructure and devolution issues.

Stephen Hill holds the Chair in Economic Development at the University of Glamorgan and is Chief Economic Advisor at the Welsh Development Agency.

Calvin Jones is a Research Associate in the Welsh Economy Research Unit. His research interests include economic deprivation in local areas and the impact of large-scale events and infrastructure developments.

Max Munday is a Lecturer in Economics and a Director of the Welsh Economy Research Unit at Cardiff Business School. He has written extensively on the effects of FDI in Wales.

David Pickernell is a Lecturer in European and International Business at the University of Glamorgan Business School.

Martin Rhisiart is a researcher at of the Observatory of Business Innovation and Development at Cardiff University.

Annette Roberts is a researcher in the Welsh Economy Research Unit. Among her research interests has been the development of Input–Output tables for the Welsh economy.

Karl Taylor is a Research Associate at the Welsh Economy Research Unit, with a specialist interest in labour economics.

Meirion Thomas is Head of the Observatory of Business Innovation and Development at Cardiff University.

1 Wales in Transition

Stephen Hill

There are many different ways of looking at the world. It would be easy to look back on the old century in Wales as one of exploitation, where mineral and human resources were systematically and ruthlessly expended in creating industrial dereliction and social exclusion (Williams, 1985). In this context the decision to grant Objective 1 status to parts of Wales, is a badge of failure: explicit recognition that turn of the century Wales has become one of the poorest parts of Europe. (Objective 1 is the highest tier of EU support to 'promote the development and structural adjustment of regions where development is lagging behind', and allows access to substantial European Social Funds to promote structural change).

An alternative approach is to look forward rather than back: to view Objective 1 funding as a new opportunity. Adding EU structural funds to the leadership potential of the National Assembly, the psychological renewal of the new century and the blossoming of a self-confident Welsh culture will present a unique combination of motivation, resources, opportunity and need (Hill and Webb, 1999).

The truth of course, is somewhere between. Economic change is not an invention of the late twentieth or early twenty-first centuries, but a continual process. Industrial economies change continuously and often very rapidly (Hill and Jones, 1999), and forecasting the economic future is much more a sophisticated art form rather than a science. The one certainty about the future is that it will be different from what we expect. Extrapolating from past changes can be appropriate in the short term, but not for much longer.

Figure 1.1 presents best estimates of the population of Wales over the past four centuries. Between 1800 and 1900 the population quadrupled, as iron-making and coal production rippled along the valleys bringing industry and people in search of a better future. This influx of people both caused and reflected changes in the structure of the Welsh economy. Figure 1.2 shows employment in key sectors over the past 150 years. Note the rapid growth in mining jobs until the 1920s and the subsequent precipitate decline: the consequent discomfort of analysts and forecasters was amongst its least important effects. Structural

1

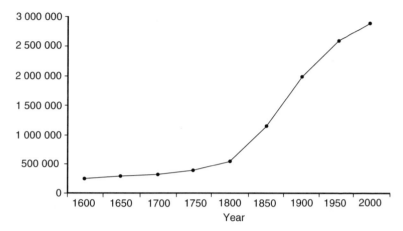

Figure 1.1 The Population of Wales, 1600–2000
Source: Hill and Jones (1999), *Welsh Economic Review*.

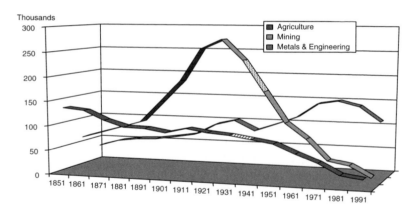

Figure 1.2 Employment in major industries, 1851–1991
Source: Hill and Jones (1999), *Welsh Economic Review*.

change is not necessarily a long-term process lasting centuries; the final 25 years saw employment in coal, iron and steel in Wales decline by over 100 000 jobs, to less than 20 000 today. Nevertheless, more steel was made in Wales in the last century than ever before, but it was made by processes that use capital rather more than people.

Table 1.1 The Welsh economy

		Wales	As % UK
Area (km^2)		20 779	8.6
Population (m)		2.92	5.0
Workforce (m)	1999	1.23	4.3
GDP (£bn)	1997	27.6	4.1
GDP/hd (£)	1997	9 442	82.2
Household income/hd (£)	1996	9 316	86.9
Unemployment rate (%)	1999	5.5	119.6

Source: Compiled from ONS, *Regional Trends*, various years.

Table 1.1 seeks to summarise the contemporary Welsh economy. Wales has 9 per cent of the UK land-mass, but 5 per cent of the UK workforce and 4 per cent of UK gross domestic product (GDP). GDP measures the sum of outputs (or, equivalently, incomes) for a defined economy over a given period (usually a year). If GDP is an appropriate measure of prosperity, then Wales is substantially less prosperous than the UK average (referred to as the 'prosperity gap'). Other prosperity indicators such as personal incomes, earnings and household incomes paint a similar, if less dramatic picture.

Table 1.2 presents a detailed picture of the composition of output in Wales in 1996, alongside the equivalent picture for the United Kingdom as a whole. The most striking differences are in manufacturing and private services. Wales has a much higher dependency on the former and a much lower dependency on the latter. Indeed, Wales is one of few European regions with a growing share of output from manufacturing over the past decade, and has a much higher dependency on manufacturing than most UK regions (Bristow, 1999).

There are many causes and consequences of this high manufacturing dependency in Wales, some of which will be considered in later chapters, but they include output growth in metal manufacturing (that is, steel and aluminium) and the continued influx of foreign direct investment (FDI) especially in electronics and engineering. Equally evident in Table 1.2 is the much lower concentration of marketed services in Wales compared to the UK average, particularly (but not exclusively) in financial and business services, alongside a slightly higher concentration in Wales of public sector services.

These relative sector specialisations turn out to have the important consequence that total output in Wales has been growing at a slower

Table 1.2   GDP by industry groups, Wales and UK, 1996

	Wales		UK	
	£m	%	£m	%
Agriculture, forestry & fishing	474	1.8	11 790	1.8
Mining, oil & gas extraction	224	0.8	4 398	0.7
Manufacturing	7 420	27.8	137 006	20.8
Electricity, gas & water	733	2.7	13 606	2.1
Construction	1 434	5.4	33 746	5.1
Marketed services (of which):	9 507	35.6	311 429	47.4
• distribution, hotels, catering & repairs	3 357	12.6	93 091	14.2
• transport & communications	1 622	6.1	54 056	8.2
• financial & business services	4 528	17.0	164 282	25.0
Non-marketed services (of which):	6 886	25.8	144 833	22.0
• public administration & defence	1 949	7.3	38 244	5.8
• education, social work & health services	4 025	15.1	81 876	12.5
• other services	912	3.4	24 713	3.8
Total	26 667	100	629 841	100

Source: Compiled from ONS, *Regional Trends*.

rate than for the United Kingdom as a whole, widening the prosperity gap. Turn-of-the-century Wales has an industrial structure that is dominated by what are, at a UK level, low-growth sectors and an equivalent under-specialisation in high-growth sectors. Hence the industrial structure of Wales is an important reason for the persistence of the prosperity gap. This is illustrated in Table 1.3.

The location quotients of columns two and three of the table are simply the ratios of each sector's share of GDP in Wales to that sector's share of UK GDP. A location quotient of more than one signifies a Welsh specialisation in that sector, whilst a figure of less than one signifies under-representation in that sector. Between 1976 and 1998, Wales became more specialised in manufacturing and public services and less specialised in private sector services, relative to the UK. The final column indexes UK sector growth rates to the UK average. Comparing the location quotients of 1998 to the indexed sector growth rates amply demonstrates the conjecture that Wales is under-represented in fast-growth sectors and over-represented in slow-growth sectors.

There is some divergence of views about how the structure of the Welsh economy will change over the next decade. Regional forecasters in general see Welsh manufacturing output as growing faster than the

Table 1.3   Concentration of Welsh industry and relative UK sector growth

	Welsh location quotients (*UK average = 1.0*)		Index of UK growth rates (*All Sectors = 100*)
	1976	*1998*	*1976–98*
Primary & energy	1.63	1.10	96
Manufacturing	0.99	1.31	52
Construction	1.15	1.18	80
Distribution, retail & catering	0.98	0.90	109
Transport & communication	0.93	0.74	195
Financial & business services	0.70	0.58	349
Public admin., education & defence	0.97	1.26	25
Other services	1.24	0.88	252

Source: Compiled from Cambridge Econometrics data.

Welsh economy average, fed by continued inward investment. However, Oxford Economic Forecasting see financial and business services in Wales as continuing to grow at a slower rate than the Welsh economy as a whole, whilst BSL (Business Strategies Ltd) take the opposite view (Table 1.4).

As noted earlier, long-term economic forecasting is an inexact process. However, neither Oxford Economic Forecasting nor BSL see Wales as making significant inroads into the relative prosperity gap, given that Table 1.4 implies annual growth rates of just 2.2 per cent and of 2.1 per cent respectively for the Welsh economy as a whole in the decade to 2007 (UK, 2.7 per cent). The prosperity gap is illustrated in Figure 1.3. Since 1987 (and before), prosperity in Wales, as measured by GDP per head, has stubbornly and persistently remained some

Table 1.4   Long-term regional forecasts of GDP growth

	Real % changes 1997–2007	
	Business Strategies Ltd	*Oxford Economic Forecasting*
Welsh manufacturing output	27.6	30.4
Financial and business services	36.6	19.4
Total Welsh GDP	23.9	22.7

Source: Bristow (1999).

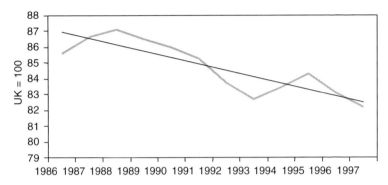

Figure 1.3   GDP per head in Wales relative to UK, plus trend-line
Source: Compiled from ONS, *Regional Trends*, various.

4–18 per cent below the UK average, with a general trend that is, if anything, downwards.

This prosperity gap has become the dominant focus of economic policy in Wales, with both the National Development Strategy (Welsh Office, 1999) and the Welsh Development Agent (WDA) Corporate Plan setting the narrowing of this prosperity gap as their primary target. Of course, agreeing targets remains easier than achieving them.

The impact of industrial structure on the Welsh prosperity gap has already been noted. A more sophisticated approach subdivides the prosperity gap into that due to activity rate differentials (the share of working-age population in, or seeking, work) and that due to productivity differentials. This is illustrated in Figure 1.4, which compares GDP per head in Wales and GDP per worker.

In 1997, GDP per person in Wales was 82 per cent of the UK average, whilst GDP per worker was 87 per cent of the UK average. The differences between GDP per worker in Wales and the UK is the productivity gap, whilst differences between relative GDP per person and GDP per worker can be attributed to the activity-rate gap – the fact that compared to the working-age population, fewer people in Wales are in or seeking work than the UK average.

This analysis then suggests that closing the activity-rate gap on the UK average would, on current figures, eliminate about one-third of the prosperity gap. Removing the productivity gap would eliminate most of the rest (but not quite all, since Wales has a slightly higher ratio of children and retired-age persons than the UK average). But, narrowing either the activity-rate or productivity gaps is easier said than done.

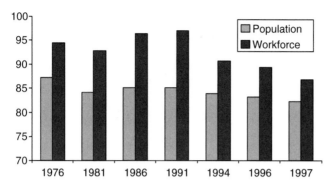

Figure 1.4 Wales GDP per head based on population and workforce
Source: Compiled from ONS, *Regional Trends*, various.

Activity rates in Wales, for both males and females, have been significantly below the UK average for most of the postwar period (although there are some signs that female activity rates are beginning to catch up). In particular, Wales has higher levels of long-term sickness (especially amongst men), and a greater proportion of persons who are early-retired. Both of these may reflect structural changes in the Welsh economy in the recent past, coupled with the relative lack of economic opportunities. Identifying and overcoming the particular obstacles that prevent people in Wales from working will be important, but so too will be increasing the volume and variety of work opportunities available.

A strategy to increase productivity will be equally long-term. The problem is not due to manufacturing, which has relatively high productivity. In 1996, average goods Value Added per head in Welsh manufacturing was £35 400, or nearly 9 per cent higher than the UK average, fed especially by high productivity in metal production, chemicals, oil-refining and transport equipment. Much of the productivity gap between Wales and the UK does, however, reflect differences in industrial structure (Table 1.2), particularly the preponderance of public sector services in Wales along with a massive under-representation of high-value-adding private sector services. As noted earlier, Wales had just 36 per cent of GDP from marketed services in 1996 compared to the UK's 47 per cent (Table 1.2). Within these, Wales was especially under-represented in the high-value-added sectors. Then the service-sector productivity problem in Wales is two-fold – relatively low levels of productivity, particularly amongst the fastest growing high-value service sectors, and a relatively lower representation in these sectors.

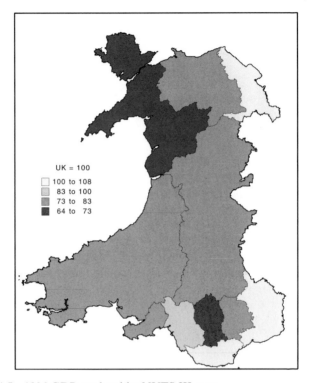

Figure 1.5 1996 GDP per head by NUTS III area
Source: ONS. (Nuts areas are the territorial units adopted by the EU for statistical purposes.)

Both are illustrated by banking and finance services in Wales, which in 1996 had a value added per worker of £33 600, compared to a UK average of £45 400. At the UK level, output of the sector grew by 78 per cent between 1981 and 1990, and by 12 per cent in the relative recession years of 1990–96, whilst corresponding Welsh figures were just 50 per cent and 3 per cent respectively (numbers from Bristow, 1999)

Identifying problems and solving them can be very different issues. Improving relative Welsh productivity means up-skilling, encouraging high-value-adding growth sectors, and encouraging people out of low-output activities into high-output ones. Each is a long-term process. The key to high value-added, high output and high wage jobs will be knowledge – not just its generation, but its commercial exploitation and application (Hill and Webb, 1999). It is increasing the knowledge intensity of work that will drive prosperity in the new century. This means putting in place the appropriate knowledge infrastructure, from nursery schools to broad-band communications, and having the motivation and skills to exploit that infrastructure.

So far, the discussion has been on an all-Wales level. In economic terms, there are many Waleses from the relatively prosperous high-output south-east and north-east corners (although each with pockets of deprivation), to the much less prosperous post-industrial areas of the south Wales valleys and the rural areas of mid and west Wales. These differences are illustrated in Figure 1.5, showing local area GDP relative to the UK average. Whilst there are some problems in interpreting workplace-based local area GDP figures, Figure 1.5 demonstrates the dispersion of prosperity across Wales.

It is the relatively low level and dispersion of GDP in Wales that has led to the granting of European Structural Fund Objective 1 status to west Wales and the valleys, opening up the prospect of some £1.3bn in structural fund support in the period to 2006. As a result, public sector economic development partners in Wales have produced a National Development Strategy, setting out potential priorities and uses for these funds. Whilst the actual uses will depend on project proposals, the emphasis is likely to be on human resource development issues rather than on physical infrastructure.

References

Bristow, G. (1999) 'Towards an Economic Analysis of Wales', Industrial Structure Sub-Group Report, May, Cardiff: WDA.

Hill, S. and Jones, C. (1999) 'Issues and Prospects for the Welsh Economy: A Long Term View', *Welsh Economic Review*, Summer p.1-3.

Hill, S. and Webb, A., (1999) *Towards a New Wales*, University of Glamorgan, Pontypridd.

Office for National Statistics (ONS) (various years) *Regional Trends*, London: HMSO.

Welsh Development Agency (1999) 'Towards an Economic Analysis of Wales', consultation document, May, Cardiff: WDA Economic Panel.

Welsh Development Agency (1999) *Promoting Prosperity: WDA Corporate Plan 2000–2003, Cardiff: WDA.*

Welsh Office (1999) *National Development Strategy for Wales*, European Task Force, Cardiff: HMSO.

Williams, G.A. (1985) *When Was Wales?*, Harmondsworth: Penguin.

2 Comparative Disadvantage? The Industrial Structure of Wales

Calvin Jones

INTRODUCTION

This chapter explores two contentions. First, that the Welsh people have a history of being in the wrong jobs at the wrong time, with employment concentrated in too few industries and occupations, often those in long-term decline. Secondly, the structure of the Welsh economy cannot currently deliver prosperity to its people. Wales' comparative disadvantage has not simply been in terms of industries and occupations, but also in the type and ownership of establishments prevalent in Wales, and the resultant nature of work. These factors have played a major part in creating an economy with low value added, low earnings and low rates of participation, as well as an unemployment rate habitually above the UK average.

The persistence of this structural disadvantage will be a major determinant of the future growth of prosperity, measured either by GDP or wider indicators of economic well-being. Equally, policy-makers seeking to create in Wales a 'vibrant, efficient and productive economy' (Welsh Development Agency, 1999, p. 2) must fully appraise themselves of Wales' current position before deciding how to reduce the prosperity gap between Wales and the UK.

The next section of this chapter will briefly describe Wales' economic history, followed by an examination of the consequences of that history, both for workers and non-workers in Wales, and also for the nature of employment. We then assess which policy areas will be crucial if Wales is to prosper in the future, presaging succeeding chapters which examine many of these policy questions in detail. The conclusion reflects upon the likelihood of success for the Welsh economy.

11

ECONOMIC HISTORY

A dominant feature of Wales' economic history since the depression has been the precipitate decline in employment in coal and steel. The sheer scale of the decline has often resulted in an under-estimation of its importance. Between 1920 and 1999, employment in mining contracted from over 300 000 to just 2000 people, mostly men (*Welsh Digest of Historical Trends*, Welsh Economy Research Unit, 1997). This devastation was compounded by a lack of diversity in employment opportunities: in 1914 over half of all employment in Wales was in coal, steel, transportation or agriculture (Williams, 1983). The succeeding depression, established well before the Wall Street Crash of 1931, delivered harsh lessons to Wales with high unemployment and stagnant output a characteristic for much of the 1920s (Rees, 1970). By the 1930s commentators could already divine the difficulties which lay ahead for the Welsh coalfields. Indeed, Marquand observed that by 1934 over half the world's shipping used oil as a power source, replacing the formerly ubiquitous coal. This long-term trend was to have disastrous consequences for the surplus labour of the coalfields, which had been encouraged by government policy to enter the industry in order to secure a strategic resource (Marquand, 1936).

Hence, government policy had failed Wales (and Britain generally) leading up to and during the depression (Rees, 1970). However, post-1945 regional development policy appeared to provide long-term solutions. Many commentators, foreshadowing the 1980s and 1990s, noted Wales's success in attracting new industries – largely manufacturing branch plants which had been established with the aid of the government (Thomas, 1962). While some dependence on coal and steel remained, diversification into heavy manufacturing had left Wales in a reasonably prosperous position by 1970. However, this represented a new dependence which, allied to the old, was to have severe consequences in the following decades.

The reduction in the manufacturing base which occurred after 1974 included not only the steel industry, but also the industrial capacity that had been painstakingly created in postwar Wales (McNabb and Rhys, 1988). Moreover, regional policy and industrial development left Wales with a structure that was ill-suited to change, and one where much control resided outside the Principality. In 1973 only a tenth of large manufacturing plants in Wales were Welsh-owned, and branch plants accounted for 70 per cent of all manufacturing employment (Tomkins and Lovering, 1973). Whether this constituted a 'dependent' economy is the subject of much debate, but some commentators have observed that such plants suffer disproportionately during economic downturns (Lovering, 1981). The decline precipitated by the oil crisis in 1973 and accelerated by government policy after 1979 had massive consequences for unemployment across the UK. In Wales, where manufacturing accounted for a third of all jobs, and where these jobs were often concentrated in small valleys communities, the shock was even greater. By 1985 the unemployment rate in Wales was 13.6 per cent, some 30 per cent higher than in the UK (Office for National Statistics). Communities which had survived the Depression were sharply reminded of the dangers of too heavy a reliance on too few industries and the vagaries of government support. The shake out in manufacturing in the 1980s had the desired effect of increasing productivity and competitiveness. However, the stock of human capital in Wales and the UK generally failed to increase, in terms of education and training, relative to its competitors (Crafts, 1993).

In Wales, most productivity gains were concurrent, not only with closure of inefficient plants, but also with increasing foreign direct investment (FDI) in manufacturing (Hill and Munday, 1993). Claims have been made that success in attracting FDI was built on the skill and adaptability of the workforce, along with the existence of major education, training and R&D facilities (Rowe-Beddoe, 1998). This is difficult to sustain, as Munday argues in Chapter 4, for while the skills and flexibility of the workforce were certainly a location factor, good road access to markets and availability of grant aid perhaps had even greater importance. Although inward investors tend to pay better than indigenous companies in Wales for equivalent occupations, and indeed productivity is higher, the functionally narrow base of many investors may have a detrimental effect on human capital development.

Hence, the Welsh economy today bears the stamp of history in terms of its industrial structure, the skills of its workforce and in the employment aspirations of the Welsh people, all of which are crucial factors governing future growth.

THE CONSEQUENCES

Industrial Structure

The manufacturing shake-out of the 1980's, together with its subsequent decline, has weakened Wales' reliance on the sector for

employment. In 1979 around a third of employment was in manufacturing, but just five years later the share had dropped to below a
quarter. Even so, in 1997 Wales remained far more dependent on
manufacturing than the UK, with the industry accounting for 22.2
per cent of employment compared with 18 per cent (ONS: *Regional
Trends*, 1985; *Annual Employment Survey*, 1999). There are both
strengths and weaknesses inherent in the relative importance of manufacturing in Wales. For example, pay in some manufacturing sectors,
particularly steel, is close to the GB average (ONS: *New Earnings
Survey*, 1998). Furthermore, manufacturing employment is generally
full-time and permanent, and relatively productive (ONS: *Annual
Employment Survey*, 1999; DTI, 1999). Meanwhile, service sector
employment in Wales is more often part-time, temporary and low
skilled, with wage rates far below the GB average (ONS: *Annual
Employment Survey*, 1999; ONS *New Earnings Survey*, 1998). Manufacturing also offers the potential benefit of supplier linkages, which are
harder to achieve in services. The principal weakness of a relatively
high dependency on manufacturing for employment lies in the threat of
competition from the less-developed world, with Wales' position as a
prime, low-cost production location within the EU under increasing
threat from Eastern Europe.

The relative share of employment in the service sector is likely to
increase in the future, hence its current nature is important. Wales has
increased employment in the financial and business services sector at a
time of decreasing employment in the UK overall, with much of this
employment occurring in call centres. However, while call centres offer
employment opportunities, and hence have been encouraged to locate
in Wales through development policies such as the South East Wales
Call Centre Initiative, the low return to the host economy may be
incompatible with increasing Welsh GDP per capita relative to the
UK. Other private service employment in Wales is also typically low-
value and low-paid. Public services in Wales are well-paid relative to
private services, and can offer highly skilled work (ONS: *New Earnings
Survey*, 1998). However, they are also subject to increasing pressure on
employment over time, and are not generally of high value added,
although this can be difficult to measure (see Hill *et al.*, 1997 who
measured the impact of the higher education sector on the Welsh
economy). These factors might suggest that an important requisite for
improving prosperity must be the development of a more 'mixed'
service economy.

Finally, despite the postwar concentration in branch plant manufacturing and more recent inward investments, Wales still lacks company headquarters and, as a corollary, research and development (R&D) activity. Subsequent efforts to attract FDI, despite government awareness of these deficiencies, have failed signally to embody this goal. Wales languishes at the bottom of the R&D league table in the UK, and there has been little evidence of change (DTI, 1999). This, and an unfavourable sectoral mix, will handicap Wales' future pursuit of prosperity.

Occupational Structure

Wales' industrial structure has resulted in an occupational mix of a generally lower order than for the UK as a whole. Taylor (see Chapter 3) observed the effect of this on wages and incomes: occupations that command less remuneration also contribute less to GDP. Wales' service sector is currently characterised by low-skill, labour-intensive employment, (Bryan *et al.*, 1997). In 1997, only 23 per cent of the Welsh workforce were engaged in managerial or professional occupations, compared to 26 per cent for the UK as a whole. Conversely, 15.5 per cent were in unskilled or other occupations, compared with 12 per cent for the UK (Welsh Office, 1999).

Occupational structure also affects the ability of an economy to respond to changing labour requirements. Two-fifths of the unemployed in Wales were formerly in unskilled occupations, largely manual labour, compared to under a third in the UK (ONS, 1999). These jobless are likely to lack qualifications, have few transferable skills, find it difficult to obtain work, and be unemployed for long periods (ONS, 1998; South Glamorgan County Council, 1994). Yet, it is difficult to see improvements for the low-skilled unemployed as the 'upskilling' of the workforce gathers pace and demand for unskilled labour falls further (Gallie and White, 1994). Reducing the numbers of 'stubborn' unemployed will be a major challenge for the future; a task further strained by the nature of industry and occupations in the Principality.

Participation

Economic restructuring in Wales over the past 25 years has changed the place, importance and nature of work for many. Differing responses to unemployment and industrial change have had a bearing on the prosperity gap between Wales and the UK, and may continue to do so for many years. In 1996 the economic activity rate in Wales, for persons of working age, was 4 per centage points below the UK average (Welsh Office, 1999). Participation rates were lower for both males and females and this discrepancy accounts for between a third and a half of Wales' GDP per capita gap with the UK. Increasing participation and employment rates are therefore a central tenet of Welsh economic policy (Welsh Office, *National Development Strategy*, 1999).

Low participation rates are an inheritance from the past. Both quantitative and qualitative evidence suggests that low male participation rates, particularly for those over 40 years of age are a vestige from the 1970s and 1980s shake-out, particularly in steel, coal and heavy industry (see Thomas, 1990; Harris, 1987 for a discussion on responses to unemployment and structural change). The Wales/UK gap in participation rates for males is particularly striking in these older age groups, comprising more permanently sick and early retired than just the unemployed (Welsh Office, 1999). This characteristic is even more marked in the South Wales valleys (OPCS, 1992). Permissive government policy allowing the older unemployed to switch to disability benefit in order to reduce the jobless total may be difficult, or impossible, to reverse (Beatty *et al.*, 1997). Furthermore, economic incentives to return to work or retrain may be negligible for those with no dependants and low housing and other costs, who have adapted over a long period to a life without work (Harris, 1987).

For those hit by economic restructuring there are more options than either complete dislocation from the labour market or re-entry with a view to finding a new permanent job. Another option is entry into the 'informal' economy. The scope and role of the informal economy in Wales, particularly in the valleys, has only been debated, yet this facet of Welsh economic life is important for several reasons (Jones, 1972; Sewell, 1975). The discreet (and difficult to measure) role of this activity within the economy may lead to inaccuracies in assessing the true nature and level of joblessness, particularly with regard to the long-term unemployed. Some long-term jobless may use their skills for economic gain, by providing services in the same fashion as a small business (Harris, 1987). Such activity is seldom a direct replacement for permanent long-term employment, but the income accrued may afford some financial stability without immediate recourse to an adverse job market or re-training. Any policy attempting to improve employment rates in Wales must give consideration to activities within the 'informal' economy.

Female participation rates in Wales are low, also as a result of past industrial structure when mining and heavy industry offered few openings. As John Williams observed,

> These formidable 'Mams', organising and ruling their houses, loving and ... feeding their progeny ... emerged not from something inherent in the character and temperament of Welsh women, but from a lack of opportunity to work outside the home.
>
> (Williams, 1983, p. 42)

In contrast to males, female participation rates are approaching the UK average as opportunities increase. However, modern barriers to female employment include a lack of childcare facilities and inflexibility of employment. Women are then more vulnerable to the 'poverty trap' given the high hidden costs of employment, which might include childcare costs; especially onerous when employment is low-paid (ERES, 1996; Shaw *et al.*, 1996). Limited career options for women in Wales may also fail to persuade many that involvement in the workforce yields sufficient rewards. Furthermore, young women with a high degree of attachment to 'place' may be less willing to relocate when their career advancement requires it, or to move speculatively to more favourable job markets (Equal Opportunities Commission, 1999).

Increasing both participation and employment rates in Wales presents a daunting challenge. However, the labour market is radically different for the young than for those in the latter part of their working life, with respect to skills, experience, economic aspirations and alternatives to work with the result that participation rates for the young in Wales are close to the national average.

Entrepreneurship

It is difficult to avoid the conclusion that low levels of entrepreneurship in Wales are a direct result of its industrial structure. From the earliest days of industry, through the 'Ironmasters' and mine owners, the postwar branch plants and to recent FDI, the Welsh have rarely owned the means of production in Wales. Even when they have, owners of the mines, ironworks and railways quickly became completely disengaged from everyday economic and social life (Morgan, 1997). Their entrepreneurial example can have had little effect upon the aspirations of the labour imported to work the mines and foundries. And decades of employment in factories and mines have left many in the Welsh workforce without family experience of entrepreneurship.

Wales performs less well than the UK in terms of VAT-registered companies per capita (see Chapter 5). Moreover, a quarter of all companies registered for VAT in Wales in 1997 were in agriculture, compared with fewer than 10 per cent for the UK as a whole (ONS 1999). In real estate and renting, finance and even manufacturing, rates of VAT registration were below the UK average. Morgan has suggested that the 'headless' occupational structure in Wales offers little scope for upward mobility through entrepreneurial activity with the result that the academically gifted in Wales have long sought outlets for their talents in public service, the arts, the church and the professions (Morgan, 1994). As Bryan comments in Chapter 5, the expectations placed upon the indigenous business sector in Wales must then be pragmatic and long-term.

THE FUTURE

Outside investment has reaped benefits for Wales, and particularly South Wales, by moderating the fall in employment associated with the decline in traditional industries. Without its success in attracting FDI, Wales may have suffered more through the recessions of the 1980s and 1990s (Welsh Office, 1998). Further, FDI has contributed to a manufacturing sector in Wales which has outperformed the UK in terms of productivity (CBI Cymru Wales, 1995). Hence, there must be some sympathy for the allure held by manufacturing and FDI for policy-makers. Yet, the case that success in FDI has led either to economic development or economic prosperity rather than simply employment growth is less easy to construct. With this in mind, an economic development policy in Wales, committed to improvement relative to the UK, must transparently account for the methods adopted in attaining its objectives.

Prioritisation

A new economic policy agenda for Wales continues apace, driven by the Assembly and the time-limited opportunity to use Objective 1 funds in the development process. However, policy targets cannot afford to create ambiguity. For example, policies aimed at simply increasing the employment rate will have a net beneficial effect on GDP whilst offering opportunities for many. However, targeting industries with high capital intensity, which also offer well-paid employment opportunities to the highly skilled while retaining profits in Wales, might yield greater returns to GDP, especially in the medium to long term. This conflict has been demonstrated by the steel industry in the 1990s, which achieved efficiency gains through capital investment and multi-skilling, while reducing the size of its workforce.

Similar conflict exists between the drive to attract FDI or encourage indigenous industries. Finite supplies of enterprise aid, human capital, education and training resources as well as prime industrial land have resulted in a tendency to favour large projects which benefit from scale economies in terms of effort and resources. The greater toil required both by smaller enterprises to win support and also for agencies to stimulate demand for support (and its subsequent administration and monitoring) implies greater inefficiencies, though the long-term benefits through diversification and enrichment of the indigenous base may be greater. Current policy pledges to continue efforts to both attract FDI and to provide the best possible support for indigenous companies (Welsh Office, 1998). Yet, the worthiest goals may be the hardest and most resource-consuming to achieve, a position that may sit uncomfortably on the impatient shoulders of policy-makers who measure time in months rather than years.

Better Services

The continuing shift towards low-value service industries poses serious problems for Wales. Wages are lowest relative to the UK (ONS; *New Earnings Survey*, 1998) and employment currently is typically low-skilled and functionally narrow in the service sector. Encouraging high value-added services is a difficult task and is unlikely to be achieved through FDI, since low wage costs in Wales and hence low unit costs is a principal attraction for such mobile services. The recent proliferation of call centres in Wales is typified by low-paid and relatively low-skilled employment, while other service sectors in Wales showing employment growth, such as personnel recruitment and security, tend to be similarly low-skill employers (ONS: *Annual Employment Survey*, 1991, 1996). Unfortunately, indigenous service sector companies currently offer little alternative to inward investment, and the base is small with only around 250 financial services companies in Wales registered for VAT. Further, whilst real estate, and renting and other business services account for 22.6 per cent of the UK VAT stock, in Wales the figure is only 12.3 per cent (ONS 1999).

This poor performance relative to the UK must be reversed if Wales is to maintain or better its position in the coming decades. However, there is no evidence that employment in the service sector in Wales in general offers any more encouragement to entrepreneurship than manufacturing. Business start-up 'triggers' such as a family example, the acquisition of suitable skills and knowledge, accessibility of capital and experience in a 'small business setting' may be just as lacking (Birley, 1998). Further, the private service sector may suffer as a result of a greater tendency for academically qualified personnel to enter public services, where Wales' stock of human capital may be the highest and for whom the rewards are greater. However, this may not be the most efficient use of human capital. The potential for addressing the effects of this balance, either through entrepreneurial role models or through improving the economic contribution of public services in Wales, is worth investigation.

Building on Existing Strengths

Although the Welsh economy suffers from many deficiencies, its social strengths are manifold, demonstrated not least by a vibrant tradition of public service, a high level of social interconnectedness, community service and family responsibility (Jones, 1972; Sewell, 1975). These strengths have yet to find economic expression with the possible exception of the illicit economy, although the near future may allow scope for such expression. The advent of Objective 1 status for Wales has brought with it EU axioms on the granting of project aid which include sustainability, the full participation of local communities, full access to opportunity and a 'bottom up' approach (West Wales European Centre, 1999). National policy-makers are slowly embracing this language and philosophy (Welsh Office, 1999). A genuine shift of the policy paradigm towards these beliefs can only benefit areas as rich in social capital as are the valleys and the rural communities of Wales (Cardiff University, 1999). It may be that working life in Wales will evolve and develop with a steady growth from the village community upwards. Further encouragement for community business, and alternative credit facilities, for example, may work a transformation, albeit in an incremental fashion.

CONCLUSION

Consecutive waves of investment in Wales from outside, from the early 'Ironmasters' and more recently from the USA, Japan and Korea, have provided a bulwark against changing global economic conditions. They have not, however, encouraged new ways of thinking about work in Wales. Nor have they persuaded the Welsh that improvements to their economic position can be generated from within the Principality. For-eign investment has been a palliative for Wales' long-term relative decline, rather than a cure. Policy should pursue opportunities for the Welsh workforce in higher-order occupations and in industries yielding the greatest return to Wales, whilst at the same time seeking to per-suade the people of Wales that the solution is self-help, not continued support. If the validity of this is accepted, the inference is that far greater discrimination must be exercised when both attracting inward investment and supporting indigenous economic activity. Measure-ments of policy achievement must reflect these subtle goals: for the modern economy the equation 'more jobs equals success' no longer holds.

References

Beatty, C., Fothergill, S., Gore, T. and Herrington, A. (1997) 'The Real Level of Unemployment', Sheffield: Hallam University.

Birley, S. (1998) 'Start Up' in P. Burns and J. Dewhurst (eds), *Small Business and Entrepreneurship*, London: Macmillan.

Bryan J., Hills, S., Munday M., Roberts, A. (1997) *Transmitting the Benefits: The Economic Impact of BBC Wales*, BBC, Cymru-Wales Cardiff.

Cambridge Econometrics (1999) 'Regional Prospects: February 1999'.

Cardiff University (1999) 'A Development Strategy for Rural Carmarthen-shire', report for Carmarthenshire Economic Development Consortium.

CBI Cymru Wales (1995) *Making it in Wales: The Way Forward for Welsh Manufacturing*, Welsh Development Agency/Touche Ross.

Crafts, N. (1993) 'Can De-industrialisation Seriously Damage you Wealth?', Hobart paper no. 120, London: Institute of Economic Affairs.

Department of Trade and Industry (1999) *Regional Competitiveness Indicators, February*, London: HMSO.

Devereux, W. (1943) 'Post War Reconstruction of Industry in South Wales', *Western Mail and Echo*, Cardiff.

Equal Opportunities Commission (1999) 'Women in Senior Management in Wales', EOC Wales.

ERES (1996) 'The Role of Women in the Welsh Workforce', Chwarae Teg, Cardiff.

Gallie, D. and White, M. (1994) *Employee Commitment and the Skills Revolution*, London: Policy Studies Institute.

Gripaios, P., Gripaios, R. and Munday, M. (1998) 'Inward Investment and City Development in the South West and Wales', in Hill S. and Morgan B. (eds), *Inward Investment, Business Finance and Regional Development*, London: Macmillan.

Harris, C. (1987) 'Redundancy and Recession', Swansea: University of Wales.

Hill, S. and Munday, M. (eds) (1993) *Inward Investment in Wales*, Cardiff: Institute of Welsh Affairs/*Welsh Economic Review*.

Hill, S. et al. (1997) 'The Impact of the Higher Education Sector on the Welsh Economy', Report for the Committee of Heads of Higher Education in Wales, Cardiff: University of Wales.

Jones M. (1972) *Life on the Dole*, London: Davis-Poynter.

Lovering J. (1981) *Dependence and the Welsh Economy*, Cardiff: UWIST Economic Research Papers.

McNabb, R. and Rhys, D.G. (1988) 'Manufacturing', in George K. and Mainwaring L. (eds), *The Welsh Economy*, Cardiff: University of Wales Press.

Marquand, H. (1936) *South Wales Needs a Plan*, London: Allen & Unwin.

Morgan, K. (1994) 'The Fallible Servant. Making Sense of the Welsh Development Agency', in Papers in Planning Research, no. 151, Department of City and Regional Planning, University of Wales, College of Cardiff.

Morgan, K. (1997) 'The Learning Region', *Regional Studies*, vol. 31(5), pp. 491–503.

Office for National Statistics (ONS) (various years) *Regional Trends*, London: HMSO.

Office for National Statistics (ONS) (1999) *New Earnings Survey, 1998* (Part E), London: HMSO.

Office for National Statistics (ONS) (1999) *Annual Employment Survey*, London: HMSO.

Office for National Statistics (ONS) (1999) *Unemployment Stocks by Occupation*, NOMIS Computer System.

Office of Population Censuses and Surveys (OPCS) (1992) *1991 Census of Population*' London: HMSO.

Office for National Statistics (1999) *VAT Registration Data*, 1997 NOMIS Computer System.

Rees, G. (1970) *The Great Slump: Capitalism in Crisis*, 1928–33', London: Weidenfeld & Nicolson.

Rowe-Beddoe, D. (1998) 'Foreword' to Hill S. and Morgan B. (eds), *Inward Investment, Business Finance and Regional Development*', London: Macmillan.

Sewell, J. (1975) *Colliery Closure and Social Change*, University of Wales Social Science Monographs.

Shaw, A. *et al.* (1996) *Moving off Income Support: Barriers and Bridges*, Department of Social Security, HMSO.

South Glamorgan County Council (1994) 'The Unemployed of Ely: Their Skills and Experience', Council report.

Thomas, B. (ed.) (1962) *The Welsh Economy: Studies in Expansion*, Cardiff: University of Wales Press.

Thomas, M. (1990) 'Coalfield Restructuring and the Enterprise Economy', PhD dissertation University of Wales, Cardiff SOCAS.

Tomkins, C. and Lovering, J. (1973) *Location, Size, Ownership and Control Tables for the Welsh economy*, Cardiff: Welsh Council.

Welsh Development Agency (1999) *Towards an Economic Analysis of Wales*, WDA *consultation document*.

Welsh Office (1998) *Pathway to Prosperity*, Cardiff: HMSO.

Welsh Office (1999) *National Development Strategy*', Cardiff: HMSO.

Welsh Office (1999) *Labour Market Assessment*, Internal Working Report.

West Wales European Centre (1999) *Objective 1 Single Programming Document*, WNEC, Corporation.

Williams, J. (1983) 'The Economic Structure of Wales since 1850', in *Crisis of Economy and Ideology: Essays on Welsh Society, 1840–1980*, Bangor: British Sociological Association.

3 Earning a Living

Karl Taylor and Jane Bryan

INTRODUCTION

Other chapters describe the role of industrial and occupational structure with particular reference to under-participation and inactivity. This chapter is more concerned with how that structure impacts on work and reward. Economic output requires a variety of inputs including both capital and people. The reward for labour inputs (earnings) is dependent on the efficiency with which these resources are brought to bear and their contribution. However, adjustments to human reward (personal earnings) also occur as a result of market fluctuations in the demand and supply of given skills in a region, with the consequence that returns for skills differ from one region to another. For example, poor supply (shortage) coupled with high demand for skilled labour in a region will result in higher returns for that labour. Equally, an over-supply of particular skills coupled with low demand would reduce their return. This, in turn, will alter perceptions of the value an individual accords to him or herself.

While the earnings structure of a region, in terms of personal incomes and regional outputs are fundamental measures of prosperity, they do not explain this prosperity. They do, however, reflect the structural mechanisms which are intrinsic to a region's wealth-creating capacity. Hence, earnings and GDP in Wales are the result of economic activity reflecting the 'industrial mix' and the occupational structure which is inherent in both the mix itself, and the quality of activity within the mix. However, the workforce, unlike other factor inputs, has almost infinite possibilities for acquiring value through productivity enhancement and skills acquisition.

The following sections will quantify and qualify the sectoral and occupational mix of the Welsh economy compared to the UK, and assess the state of the earnings component of the prosperity equation. This will be followed by a discussion of the opportunities and mechanisms involved in adding value to the Welsh workforce, emphasising that policy efforts should ensure that the structure of the Welsh economy must accommodate the product of its aspirations regarding the supply and quality of labour.

WELSH INDUSTRIAL STRUCTURE

Employment by Sector

This section highlights structural employment features of the Welsh economy compared to the UK and builds on arguments outlined in previous chapters. Table 3.1 represents a 1996 snapshot of sectoral shares of employment in Wales and the UK, and demonstrates the relative importance of each sector. For example, over a fifth of employment in Wales was in manufacturing, compared to a much smaller share for the UK as whole. Indeed, manufacturing employment in Wales increased by some 6 per cent between 1986 and 1996. This can be attributed to:

- High levels of inward investment and re-investment;
- Capital investment and productivity growth in metal manufacture;
- The integration of new SMEs into the manufacturing sector; and
- Improving price competitiveness and a growing export propensity. (Morgan and Morgan, 1998)

The table also shows that shares in public sector employment in Wales are higher than the UK, particularly in education, social services and health. Similarly, agriculture has relatively greater employment importance for Wales than the UK. Also important is the significantly lower share of financial and business service sector employment in Wales in comparison to the UK.

GDP by Sector

Table 3.2 outlines the distribution of GDP by sector in Wales and the UK for 1996. Manufacturing in Wales contributes nearly 29 per cent to Welsh GDP, compared to just over 21 per cent for the UK as a whole. Meanwhile, the public sector was responsible for 23 per cent of Welsh GDP.

Comparing Tables 3.1 and 3.2 shows that while the financial and business sector is the second largest contributor to Welsh GDP (17.4%), it has only a 10 per cent share of total employment. For the

Table 3.1   Employment shares by sector, UK and Wales, 1996

Sector	Wales (%)	UK (%)	Wales (UK = 100)
Agriculture	2.0	1.3	153.8
Mining and quarrying	0.4	0.4	100.0
Manufacturing	21.8	18.2	119.8
Energy, gas and water	0.8	0.6	133.3
Construction	3.7	3.6	102.8
Distribution	20.6	22.6	91.2
Transport	4.2	5.8	72.4
Financial & business	10.2	17.2	59.3
Public administration	8.6	6.2	138.7
Education, social services & health	22.9	19.4	118.0
Other services	4.8	4.5	106.7
Total (000s)	977	22 547	–

Source: ONS, *Regional Trends*, 1998.

Table 3.2   GDP shares by sector; Wales and UK

Sector	Wales (%)	UK (%)	Wales (UK = 100)
Agriculture	1.8	1.9	97.5
Mining and quarrying	0.9	0.7	123.5
Manufacturing	28.6	21.8	131.4
Energy, gas and water	2.8	2.2	130.7
Construction	5.5	5.4	103.1
Distribution	12.9	14.8	87.5
Transport	6.2	8.6	72.8
Financial & business	17.4	26.1	66.9
Public administration	7.5	6.1	123.6
Education, social services & health	15.5	13.0	119.2
Other services	3.5	3.9	89.5

Note: The Wales and UK columns do not total to 100% due to adjustments for financial services not shown.
Source: ONS, Regional Trends, 1998.

UK as a whole the sector contributes over 26 per cent of GDP, while employing 17 per cent of the workforce. In terms of relative scale, the sector in Wales remains underdeveloped and as demonstrated in Chapter 1, the comparison of Table 3.2 to Table 3.1 illustrates the relative productivity of different sectors – high productivity sectors contribute more to GDP than to employment and vice versa.

OCCUPATIONAL STRUCTURE

It has been noted in Chapter 1 that Wales experienced fastest growth in slow growing sectors such as manufacturing, while slower growth has been observed in the UK's faster growing sectors such as business and financial services. The next part of the discussion examines differences between Wales and the UK in terms of job quality, and changes to relative quality over time, since these drive the rationale behind economic development as opposed to growth.

The workforce of the UK and Wales is shown in Table 3.3 distributed between seven occupational categories. Higher value occupations, from professional to skilled manual employ over 68 per cent of the working population in the UK but under 62 per cent in Wales. Hence, Wales has higher shares of part-skilled, unskilled and other occupations than the UK average. The final column of the table indexes the Welsh figures and illustrates the degree of this variation from the UK average. While Wales' shares of professional and skilled manual occupations were relatively close to the UK average, more serious departures were evident in part-skilled and unskilled occupations.

Table 3.3   Occupation structure of working-age population, Spring 1997

Occupations	*Wales (%)*	*UK (%)*	*Wales (UK = 100)*
Professional	4.4	4.7	93
Manual/technical	21.9	25.2	87
Skilled non-manual	18.1	20.3	89
Skilled manual	17.5	17.8	98
Part-skilled	17.7	14.6	121
Unskilled	5.9	4.7	125
Other	14.6	12.6	115

Source: ONS, *Regional Trends*, 1998.

INDUSTRIAL AND OCCUPATIONAL EARNINGS

The foundations are now in place for consideration of how the sectoral and occupational distribution of the working population impacts on earnings in Wales. Table 3.4 allows two broad observations; first, Welsh average earnings for both sexes are substantially lower than the GB average and, secondly, the gap between Wales and the GB average is increasing over time. In 1976 average gross weekly male

Table 3.4   Average gross weekly earnings in Wales (GB = 100), 1976, 1988 and 1998

Average earnings (UK = 100)					
1976		*1988*		*1998*	
Male	*Female*	*Male*	*Female*	*Male*	*Female*
97	98.5	91.2	92.8	88.1	91.3

earnings in Wales were 3 per cent below the GB average, falling by April 1998 to over 11 per cent below of GB average. Female earnings in 1976 were 1.5 per cent below GB average, dropping to over 8 per cent below in 1998.

There are a number of viable explanations for variations in earnings, since each individual in work generates the possibility for differences to occur related to characteristics such as education, gender, work experience and so on. These differing characteristics notwithstanding, earnings would still differ across sectors and occupations and also within sectors and occupations (Taylor, 1999). However, the focus here is upon earnings differences across sectors and occupations.

Earnings by Sector

Table 3.5 shows male gross weekly earnings by sector as a percentage of the all-sector average in 1997. Manufacturing earnings in the UK were just 4 per cent below the UK all-sector average, but far above the distribution sector for which earnings are 15 per cent below. In Wales, manufacturing earnings were nearly 4 per cent above the Welsh average. That Wales has a relatively large manufacturing sector, where earnings approach the national average for the sector, which themselves approach the all-sector average, has thus been a strength.

The table also shows that financial and business services earnings in Wales are 8 per cent above the Welsh average. However, UK average earnings in finance and business service are over 27 per cent higher than the UK average. Hence, this sector, even more than manufacturing, holds attractive properties with the potential to bolster future economic output and earnings, with the result that policy-makers are understandably enthusiastic about changes to its scale in Wales.

The key to this potential lies with the quality of jobs as much as with their quantity. For example, Steel jobs in Wales are well-paid, but their

Table 3.5   Male earnings by sector as a percentage of all-sector average earnings, April 1997

Sector	Wales	UK
Manufacturing	3.8%	−4.1%
Construction	−4.0%	−8.7%
Distribution	−18.5%	−15.1%
Transport	−6.8%	−5.4%
Financial & business	8.2%	27.5%
Public administration	5.7%	3.0%
Education, social services & health	7.3%	1.6%
Whole economy earnings £ (average gross weekly wage)	363.5	407.3

Source: ONS, *New Earnings Survey*, 1997.
Note: Agriculture, mining & quarrying, energy, gas & water and construction are excluded due to small sample sizes.

numbers have diminished (Bryan *et al.*, 1994). Other manufacturing jobs in Wales have been underpinned by the 70 000 jobs in foreign-owned manufacturing units, and in terms of average *sector pay in Wales* these jobs are also well-remunerated (see Roberts, 1996). The origination of jobs is not then the issue, since there is no evidence that the aggregate indigenous effort delivers higher earnings. The notion centres firmly on the desirability of developing high-value-added sectors, *whatever their origin*, which have the potential to yield higher returns to work.

This applies equally to the service sector. As a fast growing sector in the UK as a whole, its potential in Wales has long been recognised (WDA, 1999). That this growth should take place in higher value services is the favoured course since the benefit of changes to its size in GDP and employment terms will be heavily dependent on the intrinsic quality of the employment within it. However, it has already been shown that the service sector includes a wide range of activities with varying degrees of value and returns for work. Indeed, the growth in the number of call centres in Wales has been well-publicised, and while they contribute a very small share of total employment, their relative importance to overall sector employment is set to grow. However, this type of activity may tend to offer low pay in an absolute sense, as well as being relatively low in Wales compared to elsewhere in the UK (Incomes Data Services 1999) since existing centres have a heavy reliance upon clerical and secretarial occupations, rather than the higher earnings groups. Changes to scale in important sectors should eventually provide opportunities for subsequent changes to their quality.

Earnings by Occupation

Figure 3.1 below shows earnings performance by occupation in Wales indexed to Great Britain in 1991 and 1998. Occupations are ranked in order of average pay. Hence, managers are the highest paid occupation, with pay in other occupations declining with each category. Two points are demonstrated. In 1998 earnings for managers and associate professionals in Wales were the lowest with respect to the UK average, while only the lowest paid occupations approached the GB average. Secondly, between 1991 and 1998, the earnings performance of the three highest paid occupations in Wales deteriorated relative to Great Britain whilst earnings in the middle and lower-end occupations improved. Hence, the observable trend is not favourable.

The final two columns, all non-manual and all manual occupations, shows this trend in its simplest form, with the former category experiencing declining earnings performance over time from a poor starting position, while the reverse holds for the latter. These trends over time reflect the complex relationship between supply and demand for certain skills within Wales. Improvements to the relative earnings performance

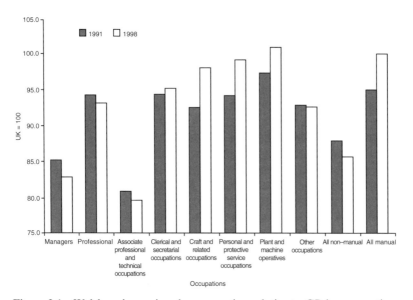

Figure 3.1 Welsh male earnings by occupation relative to GB by occupation, 1991–98

Source: Compiled from ONS, *New Earnings Survey*, 1991 and 1998 Part E.

of manual occupations over time is then a reflection of increasing demand for these activities within the economy, while the obverse is true for the higher paid occupations.

The discussion so far has attempted to illustrate and simplify the complex and simultaneous interaction between the components of prosperity; sectoral activity, occupational activity and particularly the rewards associated with them. It is apparent that the coincidence of each of these components constitutes a circular development dilemma which somehow must be broken. If the goal is high-value output, then one crucial aspect must be raising the quality of human resources in Wales.

SUPPLYING AND DEMANDING SKILLS

This development engine is a complex one, which requires that all its components are well-oiled; pristine body work is meaningless if the pistons are jammed. Similarly, policy-makers, organisations and individuals have to contrive a situation whereby skills are both supplied and demanded. Supply cannot be planned in advance of demand, or vice versa. The process, as with its effects, is indivisible. The above discussion has indicated that Wales has failed to achieve significant growth in sectors which have shown both vigour and quality elsewhere, and furthermore that growth must be stimulated in high-value activities which will then make high-value demands upon the workforce and yield high returns for that effort.

It may emerge that one of the, albeit temporary, disbenefits of restructuring, among its many benefits, is the loss of message to the workforce. In the days of coal and steel, the Welsh economy gave people clear signals regarding its requirements and the opportunities it could deliver. A dynamic economy with new ambitions and endless possibilities for diversification holds much more promise but may not yet flag up clear messages to its existing and potential workforce.

Skills shortages are perceived to be a greater constraint for Welsh employers than for those in the UK. Just under a third of employers in Wales had experienced a hard-to-fill vacancy as a result of skill shortages in 1998 (Welsh Office, 1999). However, one further penalty of modernisation has been a widening of the skills definition, which may also have diluted the collective message. For example, skills can be defined as workplace skills (organisation and working practices); formal skills (accountancy, engineering and so on); generic skills (communication, numeracy, deductive reasoning); personal attributes (leadership, initiative and so forth); and transferable skills (IT, management, sales). The Future Skills Wales project reported that 88 per cent of employers demanded good communication skills and an understanding of customer needs, while 47 per cent of employers stated a requirement for basic knowledge of IT. Only 27 per cent of employers demanded formal educational qualifications.

This may have had the effect of confusing the market between skills providers and demanders, since the skills which appear to be in most demand are either inherent, or acquired informally in the workplace and cannot be proven in advance, while only formal skills are accompanied by certificates of proof. This may well result in overconfidence among those who have gained the latter, while reducing the sense of worth (and apparent prospects) of those whose skills cannot be proved prior to employment.

The Education and Training Action Group, established by the Welsh Office in 1997, identified several key weaknesses in the Welsh labour market which are manifested in the following manner:

- One in nine pupils leave school without any GCSEs;
- Around 370 000 adults of the working-age population have no qualifications;
- Less than half of the working-age population has an NVQ3, or equivalent qualification (two A levels or an advanced NVQ);
- Over two-fifths of the working-age population have low numeracy skills; and
- One in six has low reading skills.

Attending to apparent deficiencies in formal education in Wales is an important part of the solution, but is not sufficient. Blackaby *et al.* (1999) estimated that even if the level of educational qualifications was the same in Wales as for Great Britain it would only close the earnings gap by 1 per cent. Assuming parity of Welsh occupational structure and education with Great Britain as a whole, the earnings gap would be reduced by less than 4 per cent. In 1998 the Wales/GB earnings gap for males was nearly 12 per cent (ONS, *New Earnings Survey*, 1998) and for females nearly 9 per cent (ibid). Hence an estimated 9 per cent and 6 per cent gap respectively would remain (Blackaby *et al.*, 1999). The impact of increasing educational attainment within Wales is also diluted by individuals educated in Wales taking their acquired skills elsewhere, probably attracted by higher earnings in other UK regions.

Increasing the skills level will depend on the efficiency of conduits between its supply and its demand. The first conduit must be national and local government, whose role it is to create optimism and buoyancy in the economic environment to which the suppliers and demanders of skills will respond. That message can be communicated by regarding resources devoted to people development as investment as opposed to consumption (Hill *et al.*, 1998). This means investing in higher and further education, and particularly schools, in order to remove their often 'fatigued' image. No school in Wales should have too few teachers, books, computers, classrooms or lockers. If providing adequate infrastructure is not important to its purpose, then why should the purpose be valued?

The second conduit is the job providers (the demanders of skill), who, in responding to the economic climate themselves must invoke a response among their existing and potential workforce. In the first case, employers have a duty to invest in their workforce with adequate training. In the second case, the apparent anomaly between the low priority given to formal skills and the greater focus placed on specific workplace skills would suggest that the deficit is best made good by developing strong, direct recruitment links within the education stream, starting with secondary schools. The emphasis then is for Welsh businesses to plan their skills requirements in advance and engage new entrants in their plans at the earliest possible stage. A structured, proactive and intimate response to the skills shortage would inspire optimism among the young, and call for greater discipline and strategic time investment among the skills demanders. At the same time, modern apprenticeships need to be energetically promoted to accommodate both the clear need for these practical skills in the workplace and those individuals who are better suited to vocational education.

Schools also have a role in modernising the curriculum in post-11 education, so that appropriate emphasis can be placed on general vocational competencies such as interpersonal relationships, entrepreneurship and communications skills (Hill *et al.*, 1998). They can also extend their contract with the young by meeting potential employers halfway.

In occupational terms, the preferred future economy will certainly demand more managers, professional and associate professional/technicians, the so-called knowledge workers. In the short term this will be accompanied by continued demand for plant and machinery operators, who will, however, have new demands made upon them to develop a greater range of competencies in the workplace.

CONCLUSIONS

Consideration has been given to the industrial and occupational structure of the Welsh economy in terms of employment, output and income. The manufacturing sector in Wales has not only retained its importance in terms of employment and GDP contribution, but has some favourable qualities and future potential with respect to earnings parity with the UK. Meanwhile, the finance and business sector is the largest contributor to GDP in the UK with earnings 27 per cent above the UK average. Hence, quality growth of this sector in Wales has the potential to reduce the prosperity gap.

In order to accommodate (and drive) the changing demand patterns which are inherent in such growth, the Welsh labour force must supply the necessary skills, which include formal skills but more particularly include a broad range of ever-changing multifaceted skill requirements. A successful marriage between skills supply and demand, in a rapidly changing economy, can only be achieved by direct and unambiguous engagement between the two. It will no longer be sufficient for organisations in Wales to merely identify skills shortages after the event; they must take their message into the potential workforce, into schools and colleges, marshal those resources and claim their future needs. The education system must be equally responsive. The state too can deliver a potent message through investment in the educational infrastructure and, perhaps, assist in building the necessary bridges between potential employers and employees. It only remains for the individual to be receptive to opportunity.

References

Blackaby, D., Murphy, P. and O'Leary, N. (1999) 'Income, Earnings and Prices', working draft prepared for the Welsh Development Agency, May 1999, Swansea University.

Bryan, J., Hill, S., Munday, M. and Roberts, A. (1994) *Steel in Wales: The Economic Impact of Steel Production in Industrial South Wales*, Standing Conference on Regional Policy in South Wales, July 1994.

Hill, S., Roberts, A. and Miller, N. (1998) 'The Welsh Workforce', chapter 17 in J. Osmond (ed.), *The National Assembly Agenda*, Cardiff: Institute of Welsh Affairs.

Incomes Data Services (1999) *Report No. 793*, 1999 London: 105.

Morgan, B. and Morgan, K. (1998) 'Economic Development', chapter 13 in J. Osmond (ed.), *The National Assembly Agenda*, Institute of Welsh Affairs.

Office for National Statistics (ONS) (various years) *Regional Trends*, London: HMSO.

Office for National Statistics (ONS) (various years) *New Earnings Survey*, London: HMSO.
Roberts, A. (1996) 'The Economic Impact of Foreign Manufacturing Investment in Wales', PhD dissertation, University of Wales, Cardiff.
Taylor, K. (1999) 'Male Earnings Dispersion over the Period 1973–1995 in Four Industries', Working Paper no. 99–021, Cardiff Business School.
Welsh Development Agency (1999) *Towards an Economic Analysis of Wales*, Industrial Structure sub-group report, May, Cardiff: WDA.
Welsh Office (1999) *Future Skills Wales*, Cardiff: HMSO.

4 Foreign Direct Investment in Wales: Lifeline or Leash?

Max Munday

INTRODUCTION

The 1980s and 1990s have seen increasing global debate about the regional contribution of foreign-owned manufacturing. In Wales, one context of this debate has been why, following an extended period of 'spectacular' inward investment successes, Wales has continued to have such disappointing figures on indicators of economic well-being in relation to other UK regions. This chapter begins with a review of the 'facts' on foreign direct investment in Wales, focusing on the differences between the foreign-owned and domestically owned manufacturing sector, and on recent development trends in the foreign manufacturing sector. We then explore a selection of the issues that surround the presence of foreign manufacturing in Wales, particularly in terms of the contribution of the sector to regional development processes. The final section contains conclusions which explore the likely trajectory of the foreign-owned manufacturing sector in Wales, largely in the context of expected changes in the location competitiveness of Wales and the UK.

THE 'FACTS'

It is first necessary to be clear on what is meant by foreign direct investment (FDI). FDI is defined as 'investment abroad by an individual or firm with the objective of obtaining ownership and influence over income generating assets' (Eurostat, 1998). The definition is important. In considering the activities of multinational enterprises in Wales there may be a tendency to think in terms of new investors on greenfield sites. Certainly it is this type of investment, typified by the cases of LG (Newport) and Toyota (Deeside), that generates most publicity. However, the definition also includes acquisitions of domestic firms by foreign ones – activities not always recognised by the press or regional development agencies – particularly where an English-based parent company of a Welsh branch plant is taken over by a foreign company. This point is worth making because cross-border mergers and acquisitions make up an increasing proportion of global FDI flows. Moreover, the role of acquisitions by foreign firms in the growth of the foreign manufacturing sector in Wales, and elsewhere, has generally been underestimated (Stone and Peck, 1996). The above definition of FDI also covers inward investment into services sectors, which have received limited attention in Wales because of the paucity of reliable data. However, foreign-owned services companies probably employ as many people in Wales as foreign-owned manufacturing – good cases include the major hotel chains, petrol service stations and recent investments in financial and business services (see also Gripaios and Munday, 2000).

The focus of this chapter is, however, foreign-owned manufacturing, and to some extent, the 'facts' here are also obscured by the ambiguity of much of the data (Hill and Munday, 1994; Stone and Peck, 1996). The UK Census of Production provides estimates of employment, gross value added, and capital spending in the foreign-owned manufacturing sector in Wales, whilst the Welsh Register of Manufacturing Employment (from the Welsh Office) publishes data on foreign manufacturing employment, size and sources of foreign holding. Finally, the Welsh Development Agency provides some information on the number of new foreign projects and associated employment. Estimates of the size of the foreign-owned manufacturing sector differ significantly between the main sources. For example, in 1996 the Census of Production reported around 58 000 employed in the foreign-owned manufacturing sector, with the Welsh Register of Manufacturing Employment reporting around 75 000. Part of the discrepancy may be due to the fact that the Census fails to fully recognise the extent of foreign acquisition of domestic firms. However, even this larger number may be an under estimation with, for example, the Welsh Register tending to consistently underestimate employment in the Asian manufacturing sector (see Morris *et al.*, 1993).

As a consequence of the above, the actual extent of foreign ownership of Welsh manufacturing and services is unknown. From the point of view of policy-making within the new National Assembly, and the large amounts of money that are spent in marketing Wales to foreign companies, the poor quality of information could be usefully remedied.

How important is this information, and why should there be an interest in the facts about the foreign-owned sector? For example, it may be argued that inward investment should include UK companies controlled from outside the Principality, and, indeed, many of the criticisms levelled at the foreign-owned sector may be equally applicable to the large number of UK-owned 'branch plants' in Wales (see Welsh Affairs Committee, 1988).

One reason for more careful scrutiny of the foreign-owned sector is that it is 'different' from UK-owned branch plants in Wales, and from indigenous Welsh manufacturing. Foreign-owned manufacturers in Wales are often subject to different constraints, and are able to access wider opportunities than the domestic manufacturing base which contains large numbers of smaller firms which are not international in scope. Differences in operational context and scope have ramifications for the contribution of such multinational firms to the regional economy. Large parts of the foreign manufacturing base in Wales exist within an international division of labour. For the modern multinational, organising design, production, purchasing, sales and distribution on a national (or even continental) basis can be inefficient. Rather, such firms can maximise opportunities to organise operations globally, so that an apparently large production plant in Wales may be a very small part of a global jigsaw of operations. The foreign firm may also have greater opportunities to shift production between locations to take advantage of international differences in factor costs.

Foreign firms are different in other ways. Theory explaining the growth of the multinational enterprise suggests that such firms possess certain 'ownership advantages' which compensate for the additional costs involved in overseas production. These superior assets, whether tangible or intangible, perhaps in terms of patents, managerial expertise, technology or knowledge, can result in greater efficiency than their domestically-owned counterparts (see Dunning, 1993). There is evidence to support this contention. For example, Davies and Lyons (1992) found that foreign-owned manufacturing in the UK had a 40 per cent productivity advantage over domestic firms, which could only partly be explained by their concentration in capital-intensive sectors. Evidence from Wales also supports the notion of superior performance in the foreign sector. Table 4.1 shows labour productivity (and average earnings) by selected industry sectors in Wales by source of ownership. The foreign productivity advantage is particularly noticeable in the metals and electronics sectors. Other evidence of such productivity differences comes from Munday and Peel (1998) who analysed the relative performances of matched samples of foreign and domestic firms in Wales (matched on age, industrial classification and size) between 1989 and 1992. They reported similar differences in productivity (see Table 4.2) – those differences being reflected in higher levels of pay in the foreign sector.

In summary, foreign firms in Wales tend to be significantly larger, more productive and higher paying than domestic firms. Such productivity differences are important, because part of the rationale for attracting foreign capital to the UK is that such relatively productive inward investors might provide a stimulus to the domestically-owned sector, perhaps through the demonstration of new methods of work organisation, technology transfer, or other spillovers. For example, Barrell and Pain (1997) estimated that around 30 per cent of the productivity growth in UK manufacturing in the decade to 1995 could be

Table 4.1   Labour productivity by industry in Wales, 1995

	Labour productivity		Average gross salary	
Sector	*UK manufacturing*	*Foreign manufacturing*	*UK manufacturing*	*Foreign manufacturing*
Rubber etc.	69 843	87 138	16 567	19 728
Metals	102 974	221 783	20 712	23 396
Engineering	52 680	78 735	17 726	21 567
Electronics	58 806	110 747	16 023	19 035
Trans. eqmt etc.	90 195	128 897	19 982	22 842
Average	81 436	126 457	18 686	20 850

Source: Brand *et al.* (1999).

Table 4.2   Foreign and domestic manufacturing characteristics in Wales, 1992

	Foreign firms mean (median)	*Domestic firms mean (median)*
Employment 1992	281.4 (165.0)	194.3 (99.5)
Average remuneration (£)	15 396 (15 362)	13 758 (13 940)
Sales per employee (£)	88 091 (72 726)	59 884 (52 571)

Note: Number of observations, employment $n = 76$ foreign, and $n = 88$ domestic; remuneration $n = 78$ foreign, $n = 87$ domestic; sales per employee $n = 68$ foreign, $n = 85$ domestic.
Source: Munday and Peel (1998).

associated with the impact of inward investment. The 'ripple through' effects of changes in production and working practices triggered by the presence of new inward investors were seen to have been particularly important.

FDI has a long history in Wales; the earliest foreign manufacturing company to enter Wales (Monsanto) arrived in 1895. The USA dominated inward investment inflows into Wales until the 1970s. Postwar US investments into Wales largely represented either completely new greenfield investments or relocations from the south-east of England. In many cases, location choices reflected the need to access UK and European markets for income-elastic consumer products. The share of European and Japanese manufacturing investment in the Welsh total increased dramatically after the 1970s, largely in line with the greater role that these areas have played in global FDI flows. By 1974, foreign-owned manufacturing companies employed an estimated 53 000 people (around 16 per cent of Welsh manufacturing employment at that time), and had invested approximately half a billion pounds in Wales. In 1974, around 90 per cent of foreign manufacturing in employment terms was in North American firms. Table 4.3 reveals that US investment is still an important component of the foreign-owned manufacturing sector in Wales.

The foreign-owned sector in Wales was not immune from the general shake-out in Welsh manufacturing that occurred after 1980. By 1984, foreign-owned manufacturing employment had fallen to around 40 000, but has risen steadily since then, reaching an estimated 75 000 by 1996 (ONS, 1998). A key constituent of recent growth has been the Asian sector, where employment at the end of 1999 had reached over 20 000, rivalling the EU as a source of inward investment into Wales. Figure 4.1 provides an index of employment and real output growth in the foreign-owned sector, together with an index of growth in domestic manufacturing employment in Wales. It reveals that employment and output in the foreign-owned manufacturing sector in Wales has been stable compared to the domestic sector. However, upward trends in foreign-owned manufacturing employment may simply reflect a transfer from the domestic to the foreign-owned sector – an issue to be addressed later.

The largest proportion of employment is in the electrical equipment and electronics sector (Figure 4.2), where again large investments by Asian firms such as Sony, Matsushita, Sharp, LG, Acer and Hitachi add much to the total. Another large sector is automotive components led by firms such as Ford, Calsonic, TRW and Toyota. Some of the

Table 4.3 Foreign-owned companies in Wales: enterprises and employment

	Number of enterprises			Employment (000s)		
	1981	1988	1996	1981	1988	1996
USA	77	98	116	31.0	26.6	30.9
Canada	4	9	12	4.3	3.6	3.0
EU	23	66	123	3.9	7.6	20.2
Australia	8	9	Not sep. listed	1.3	0.5	Not sep. listed
Japan	Not sep. listed	15	28	Not sep. listed	6.9	16.9
Sweden	Not sep. listed	13	Inc. in EU	Not sep. listed	1.7	Inc. in EU
Switzerland	7	10	9	1.1	1.3	0.9
Other	25	18	26	3.8	0.8	1.8
Total	144	236	314	45.4	51.3	75.4

Source: Compiled from ONS, *Welsh Economic Trends* and *Digest of Welsh Statistics*, various years.

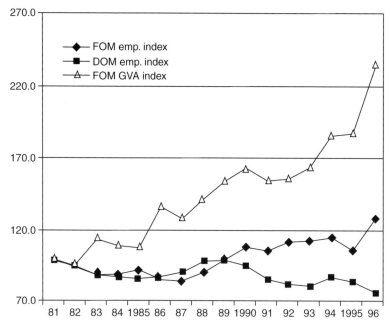

Figure 4.1 Index of foreign manufacturing employment and gross value added in Wales, 1981–96 (1981=100)
Source: Derived from ONS *Census of Production.* Table PA1002, various years.

largest foreign investments in capital terms (although not in terms of employment) are in chemicals and process sectors – including Texaco, Dow Corning, and Associated Octel.

Wales has been comparatively successful in attracting foreign direct investment. Hill and Munday (1994) calculated that between 1982 and 1992, Wales attracted 545 foreign projects (including acquisitions, joint ventures and greenfield ventures) with associated planned or safe-guarded employment of 37 000. Wales effectively collected around 16 per cent of the foreign projects coming to the UK during the period. The Department of Trade and Industry has since ceased to provide regional details of planned and safeguarded employment in new pro-jects because these were being manifested in 'misleading' league tables of regional FDI success. However, details of new projects are still available, and Wales continues to receive a relatively high share. For example, between 1993 and 1997 Wales attracted 179 new foreign projects – some 14 per cent of the UK total in the period.

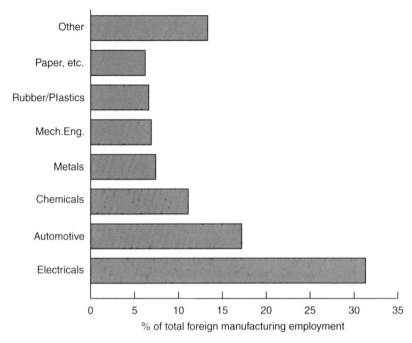

Figure 4.2   Activities of foreign manufacturers in Wales, 1996
Source: Derived from Welsh Office, *Digest of Welsh Statistics*, 1997.

Different foreign manufacturers have different location criteria. However, empirical evidence has suggested that relative Welsh success in attracting inward investment can be explained in terms of low unit labour costs, good road infrastructure and access to grants and other financial assistance (Hill and Munday, 1994). Much of the recent inward investment into Wales has been concentrated in south-east and north-east Wales, from where there is good road infrastructure to the main UK consumer markets, and further to Europe. Furthermore, Wales contained Assisted Areas where new locators could gain access to financial assistance. Importantly, these were fairly close to the large consumer markets in the south-east of England – this often being a factor in new location decisions. The conclusion is that multinationals enter Wales to take advantage of favourable regional production conditions (low unit labour costs, and access to labour), whilst maintaining access to key consumer markets. Such location criteria have important ramifications for the role of such subsidiaries in present and future economic development processes (Phelps, 1997).

In conclusion, the foreign manufacturing sector in Wales has grown in significance; *prima facie* this would appear good news for Wales. The typical foreign investor is larger, more productive, higher paying, and probably more stable than its domestic counterpart. Moreover, during the 1980s, foreign multinationals succeeded in diversifying the regional manufacturing base at a time of structural upheaval, created new direct and indirect employment, and provided a boost to local incomes and spending. Equally, foreign multinationals have been associated with demonstration effects in terms of industrial relations practices, work organisation and technology/knowledge transfer to local suppliers (see Morris *et al.*, 1993; Munday *et al.*, 1995). In the context of so much good news about FDI in Wales why does the debate on the contribution of the sector to economic development remain active?

THE 'ISSUES'

This section reviews some of the issues surrounding the growth and contribution of foreign-owned manufacturing in Wales. More detailed treatments are found in Lovering (1998), Gripaios (1998), Munday *et al.* (1995) and Phelps (1997).

The attraction of foreign manufacturing as a means of strengthening regional prospects is increasingly seen as just one among a series of development alternatives. The emphasis on the attraction of foreign capital, particularly during the 1970s and early 1980s, should be seen in the context of structurally related decline, high regional unemployment and a yawning gap in new domestic investment in Wales (see Davies and Thomas, 1976). During this period there appeared to be few real alternatives to the 'inward investment model' of development. Latterly, however, the longstanding debate centering on the true costs of attracting foreign capital has gathered momentum (see Christodoulou, 1996 for a review). Debate has not focused solely on the explicit costs of attracting foreign firms in terms of grants and infrastructure, but also on the implicit costs of the inward investment model in terms of opportunities foregone. As the real resources available for development in Wales have fallen, some have argued that scarce resources might be as well used in developing the indigenous enterprise base, supporting the development of supply clusters and promoting endogenous growth within the framework of a more innovative and learning region (Morgan, 1997).

Although regional development resources are being channelled in new directions, Wales will enter the new millennium with the attraction of foreign direct investment still very much at the forefront of actual policy. Great efforts are still expended to extract new investment from the internationally mobile manufacturing pot. Long and often acrimonious interregional battles to attract investments, such as LG (Newport) and Acer (Cardiff), provide ample evidence of this. Longer-term local development still hinges on the transforming powers of comparatively productive inward investors, although the precise mechanisms through which better productivity and technology are carried over into indigenous sectors are still poorly understood. Lovering (1998) examining the role of FDI in Wales, showed that one questionable focus of present policy is the role of multinationals as a catalyst for the development of regional clusters generating the static benefits of reduced costs, and the dynamic benefits of a collective commitment to innovation, 'which is now ubiquitously seen as the key to both corporate and regional competitiveness' (Lovering, p. 7). Unfortunately, and as Lovering aptly demonstrates, there is very little evidence on levels of embeddedness of foreign investors in Wales. The larger scale development of clusters along the Porter (1990) model is only a distant possibility in the new millennium, and likely to be hindered by the low underlying economic activity base in the region. Perhaps more fundamentally, it should not be forgotten why foreign firms enter Wales; access to relatively low-cost and productive labour, and proximity to markets. Although incoming firms undoubtedly benefit from locally-based components supply infrastructure, this is a low priority compared to keeping other production costs as low as possible.

This factor prompts consideration of a related issue – foreign manufacturing plants in Wales usually only manufacture or assemble, rather than undertake higher order functions. The Welsh Affairs Committee (1988) reported that:

> The results of surveys of inward investors in Wales showed that although there was some developmental work at plant level there was little in the way of larger scale, more fundamental R&D work...[plant] autonomy was generally limited, few plants had any higher management functions, and most were controlled from a headquarters outside the Principality.

The above characterised the 1980s and there is very little evidence to suggest that much has changed in the 1990s. A narrow functional base in subsidiaries can restrict employment opportunities, and at a regional level can contribute to a low skills equilibrium that damages long-term development prospects. There are notable exceptions to the above; for example, in the Asian manufacturing sector firms such as Sony, Calsonic and Yuasa each report having research and development activity in Wales. However, many of these firms actually undertake development work or engineering as opposed to basic or applied research as defined by the *Frascati Manual* (see Morris *et al.*, 1993). Of course, the 'production only' basis of Welsh operations equally applies to many UK-owned branch plants resident in the region. However, the 'production-only' emphasis and the 'cost-down' location criteria of the foreign sector, when combined with their potentially greater mobility and flexibility, raises concerns about the stability of these firms, particularly those producing standardised products at the mature phases of life-cycles, who by virtue of their greater global reach have the best opportunities to produce in lower cost supply points when conditions are right (Vernon, 1971; McAleese and Counahan, 1979).

The employment index in Figure 4.1 suggests that this issue of stability is little cause for concern, and that, in fact, the foreign sector is more stable than the domestic sector, and it is the latter where the concern should be. However, closer inspection of recent changes in foreign-owned manufacturing employment in Wales reveals that some of the comparative stability in the sector is, in fact, illusory and caused by foreign acquisitions of indigenous enterprises. Table 4.4 reveals that, between 1979 and 1993, closures and divestments together with contractions of operations actually led to the loss of nearly 35 000 jobs in foreign-owned enterprises, whilst acquisitions accounted for the safeguarding of nearly 20 000 jobs. In overall terms the foreign-owned manufacturing sector may not then be as stable as the total employment figures suggest. Moreover, Table 4.4 reveals that one of the most significant additions to new employment has come from the Asian manufacturing sector, and this is currently an uncertain sector with respect to employment prospects because of the fall-out from the Asian currency crises, and the drawn-out adjustment phase in the Japanese domestic economy (see Munday *et al.*, 1999).

Concerns about longer-term trends in global FDI outflows, together with increasing competition to host such investment, have led some to conclude that resources in Wales (and other UK regions) might be better used in improving the embeddedness of existing foreign investors. Embeddedness is multifaceted, but one important measure is the extent to which enterprises are backwardly linked into the regional

Table 4.4 Employment changes in foreign-owned manufacturing enterprises in Wales, 1979–93

	Initial stock @ 1979	New creations	Closures	Acquisitions	Divestments	Expansions	Contractions	Net change	Stock @ 1993
USA	40700	5000	4900	9400	9300	2100	11600	−9400	31300
EC	5600	2700	1000	8000	100	1000	1500	+9000	14600
Non-EC Europe	3600	1500	500	2000	1900	900	500	+1500	5100
Japan	2700	6900	n.a.	n.a.	n.a.	n.a.	n.a.	+8500	11200
Other	6200	800	300	n.a.	1000	n.a.	na	−400	5800

Note: n.a. = not available at this level of disaggregation. Some changes in stock may not add up because of rounding.
Source: Derived from Stone and Peck (1996).

supply base. The level of backward linkages is related to the nature and quality of indirect employment creation, and potentially provides a transactional context for the transfer of technology and knowledge from the foreign sector to the local manufacturing sector. Hirschmann (1958) shows that industries with low levels of backward linkages often contribute least to regional growth prospects.

How well is the foreign manufacturing sector in Wales linked to the local supply base? Roberts (1996) considered both the backward and forward linkages created by foreign-owned manufacturing firms in Wales, and reported that less than 17 per cent of non-wage spending actually occurred in the region. Gripaois and Munday (2000) report the poor state of linkages between inward investors and the locally-based financial and business services base in Wales. Table 4.5 shows that the foreign-owned manufacturing sector generally purchases less within Wales than does the domestic sector. This may reflect the comparative importance of intra-corporate trade in the foreign manufacturing sector, as well as the fact that foreign manufacturers in Wales have a greater 'reach' in sourcing, and may also comprise a small part of supply chains which are organised on a global basis to maximise scale and scope economies.

Where purchasing is organised globally the potential for local suppliers may be reduced (Phelps, 1993). There are some notable exceptions in Table 4.5 with the foreign-owned transport equipment sector buying more locally than its domestic counterpart. This could reflect several factors. First, some of the larger motor components makers in the region purchase considerable amounts from other foreign producers in the region. Further, the foreign-owned transport equipment sector is well-established in the region and has fully explored local

Table 4.5 Percentage of materials and services sourced in host region, 1995

	Wales	
	UK manufacturing	*Foreign manufacturing*
Rubber and plastics etc.	33.6	28.4
Metals	30.9	24.5
Engineering	35.3	27.0
Electronics	35.1	25.2
Trans. equipment etc.	28.6	33.3
All Welsh manufacturing	31.5	

Source: Derived from Brand *et al.* (1999).

purchasing opportunities; and finally the region is beginning to benefit from the clustering in the motor components sector in industrial South Wales. However, the overall evidence on backward linkages is disappointing, and one issue facing policy-makers is how far such linkages can be improved on the small economic activity base that Wales represents.

Finally, issues arise concerning the growing dependence of Wales on foreign capital. An increasing proportion of the Welsh manufacturing base has become foreign-owned over time. In 1981, 23 per cent of Welsh manufacturing employment and 36 per cent of manufacturing gross value added was generated in the foreign sector. By 1996, the comparator figures were 39 per cent and 43 per cent respectively. In the context of Table 4.4, mergers and acquisitions have had a strong bearing on these figures. Paradoxically, whilst the creation of the National Assembly, in theory, provides scope for a greater level of political and economic decision-making within Wales, it is also the case that a growing number of the most important decisions affecting Welsh industry are taken abroad, far distant from the local context. Consequently trends in foreign ownership have exposed the Welsh economy more and more to global events, while making Wales less dependent on the state of UK markets, and this trend is set to continue. Moreover, the truncated nature of decision-making within foreign plants, coupled with what is largely a 'production-only' operations base raises important questions of technical dependence in what has been characterised as a learning region.

CONCLUSIONS: THE FUTURE

One of central issues facing policy-makers in the future will be that despite attracting relatively large amounts of foreign capital in the last few decades, Wales remains at the end of the century one of the poorest regions of the UK (Brand *et al.*, 1997). It is still difficult to make a case for well-publicised inward investment successes leading to sustained improvements in indicators of economic well-being, although Wales might have been even poorer without the inward investment. But what of the longer-term prospects for foreign-owned manufacturing in Wales, and will the future be as the past?

The future of manufacturing FDI into Wales first needs to be seen in the context of global patterns in FDI flows – flows which can be difficult to predict. It also needs to be seen in terms of factors affecting the location competitiveness of the UK and its regions. Foreign direct investment, rather than exports, is likely to remain the dominant means by which multinational enterprises serve international markets. The global FDI stock was estimated to have reached $3.5 trillion in 1997, around double its value in 1990, and FDI flows show no signs of slowing, although cross-border mergers and acquisitions have played a more significant role in flows during the later 1990s (UNCTAD, 1998). Within Europe, the UK maintains its strong position as the main destination of inward FDI, typically accounting for around one-fifth of investment into and between the EU per annum (although much of this investment is in financial and business services, as opposed to manufacturing – see Eurostat, 1998).

The factors expected to influence FDI manufacturing inflows into Wales are to a large extent those which will influence flows to the UK into the next millennium, and include:

- The strength of the global, and particularly the US and Japanese economies. Outside of the EU these remain the two most important sources of inward investment in Welsh manufacturing.
- The speed of recovery in Southeast Asia following the currency crises and general 'meltdown' of 1997 and 1998. The UK had focused marketing efforts there and it was regarded as one of the most probable sources of new inward investment. While Wales has won some inward investment from Southeast Asia, these flows have now been sharply eroded, and are unlikely to pick up in the initial part of the new millennium.
- The growing location competitiveness of Central and Eastern Europe – in particular Poland, the Czech Republic and Hungary. Manufacturing inward investment into these areas has increased sharply during the 1990s, and this trend is expected to continue (see for example ERECO, 1999).
- The reaction of inward investors to the UK's 'position' on the single currency, with some large investors already voicing concern about the UK's commitment to a federal Europe.
- The economic policy adopted by the UK government. For example, a strong pound is expected to moderate inward investment prospects in the shorter term, while the weaker euro could improve the international location competitiveness of European mainland areas.
- The ongoing processes of restructuring within multinational enterprises in response to the opportunities offered by the European single market.

Where does all of this leave Wales? The growing competition to attract inward investment, triggered by the expansion of the European Union, appears likely to affect the volume of inward FDI inflows into Wales. To this is added the threat of more institutional competition to attract FDI from the new English regional development agencies. The competitive advantages of Wales as an inward investment location are still found in relatively productive labour coupled to market accessibility and financial aid. This type of competitive advantage is slowly being eroded, and more so as several years of high sterling hit exporters' competitiveness. This loss of international competitiveness is already being reflected in the recent shifts of foreign manufacturers' operations to the Far East and Eastern Europe (see Munday *et al.*, 1999).

Coupled to these trends is the reduction in the real level of resources to market Wales as an industry location. Much of this points to the fact that a boom in new inward investment into Wales, as occurred during the late 1980s led by the Japanese, is unlikely to be repeated in the foreseeable future.

Wales will do well if it can maintain its employment in foreign manufacturing industry at the current level. The decade to 2010 will undoubtedly witness some spectacular closures amongst the older foreign investors producing standardised, mature or processed products well into the decline stage of the cycle. Counterbalancing growth is expected to come more from expansions within existing investors, as opposed to large new greenfield projects, with the electronics engineering and motor components sectors leading the way, much as they have done during the 1990s. Whilst regional development organisations in Wales may exert little influence on the nature of incoming foreign manufacturing operations, growing factor constraints in the northeast and south-east of Wales may result increasingly in the siting of new projects in the west of the Principality. This shift may be further aided by areas taking advantage of their new Objective 1 status, with the result that the benefits of such inward investment will at least be better distributed.

The debate on the precise nature of the contribution of foreign manufacturing looks set to roll on. Although the terminology of the debate has changed, many of the issues outlined above are identical to those which permeated the general 'branch plant syndrome and embeddedness' debate for many years. Although commentators and policy-makers have identified a need to target marketing resources on those foreign sectors adding most to regional value added, the reality is that Wales will continue to attract what it can in an increasingly competitive market to win internationally mobile capital projects. This was made particularly evident in one of Wales' recent inward investment successes:

> One hundred and fifty jobs will be created by a Chinese company in a Welsh unemployment blackspot... the factory... will be called Leaveland Shoe Co. Ltd. It will assemble shoes and distribute them across the UK... Pembrokeshire found itself on a shortlist of three – including Poland and Namibia – to be the company's bridgehead into Europe.   (Jones, 1998)

There is very little to suggest that the immediate future will differ from the past.

References

Barrell, R. and Pain, N. (1997), 'FDI and Economic Growth within Europe', *Economic Journal,* vol., pp. 1770–86.

Brand, S., Hill, S., Munday, M, and Roberts, A. (1997) 'Why Isn't Wales Richer? Economic Change and GDP per capita', *Local Economy*, vol. 12(3), pp. 219–33.

Brand, S., Hill, S. and Munday, M. (1999) 'Assessing the Impacts of Foreign Manufacturing to Regional Economies: The Case of Wales, Scotland and the West Midlands', Cardiff Business School/Plymouth Business School, working paper.

ERECO (1999) *European Sectoral Prospects*, Cambridge: Cambridge Econometrics.

Christodoulou, P. (1996) *Inward Investment: An Overview and Guide to the Literature,* London: British Library.

Davies, S. and Lyons, B. (1992) 'Characterising Relative Performance: The Productivity Advantage of Foreign-owned Firms in the UK', *Oxford Economic Papers*, vol. 43, pp. 584–95.

Davis, G. and Thomas, I. (1976) *Overseas Investment in Wales*, Swansea: C. Davies.

Dunning, J. (1993) *Multinational Enterprises and the Global Economy*, Reading: Addison Wesley.

Eurostat (1998) *European Union Direct Investment: Yearbook 1997*, Luxembourg: Office for Official Publications of the European Communities.

Gripaios, P. (1998) 'The Welsh Economy: An Outside Perspective', *Contemporary Wales*, vol. 10, pp. 32–49.

Gripaios, P. and Munday, M. (2000) 'Uneven Development in Financial Services: The Case of Wales and the South West', *Service Industries Journal*, forthcoming.

Hill, S. and Munday, M. (1994) *The Regional Distribution of Foreign Manufacturing Investment in the UK*, London: Macmillan.

Hirschmann, A. (1958) *The Strategy of Economic Development*, New Haven, Conn.: Yale University Press.

Jones, C. (1998) 'Chinese Bringing Factory to Welsh Jobs Blackspot', *Western Mail*, 2 November.

Lovering, J. (1998) *Misreading and Misleading the Welsh Economy: The 'New Regionalism'*, Papers in Planning Research, Dept. of City and Regional Planning, University of Cardiff.

McAleese, D. and Counahan, M. (1979) 'Stickers or Snatchers? Employment in Multinational Corporations during the Recession', *Oxford Bulletin of Economics and Statistics,*, vol. 41, November, pp. 345–58.

Morgan, K. (1997) 'The Learning Region: Institutions, Innovation and Regional Renewal', *Regional Studies*, vol. 31(5), pp. 491–503.

Morris, J., Munday, M. and Wilkinson, B. (1993) *Working for the Japanese,* London: Athlone.

Munday, M., Morris, J. and Wilkinson, B. (1995) 'Factories or Warehouses – a Welsh Perspective on Japanese Transplant Manufacturing', *Regional Studies*, vol. 29, pp. 1–17.

Munday, M. and Peel, M. (1998) 'The Comparative Performance of Foreign-owned and Domestic Manufacturing Firms during Recession: Some Descriptive Evidence from Wales', *Contemporary Wales*, vol. 10, pp. 50–80.

Munday, M., Pickernell, D. and Roberts, A. (1999) *The Asian Crises and Foreign Direct Investment: Some Welsh Perspectives*, paper for Regional Studies Association European Conference, Bilbao, Spain, September.

Office for National Statistics *Manufacturing, Product and construction Inquiries*, HMSO: London, various years.

Phelps, N. (1993), 'Branch Plants and the Evolving Spatial Division of Labour: A Study of Material Linkage Change in the Northern Region of England', *Regional Studies*, vol. 27, pp. 87–101.

Phelps, N. (1997) *Multinational and European Integration*, London: Jessica Kingsley.

Porter, M. (1990) *The Competitive Advantage of Nations*, New York: Free Press.

Roberts, A. (1996) 'The Economic Impact of Foreign Manufacturing Investment in Wales', PhD thesis, University of Wales.

Stone, I. and Peck, F. (1996) 'The Foreign-owned Manufacturing Sector in UK Peripheral Regions, 1978–1993: Restructuring and Comparative Performance', *Regional Studies,* vol. 30(1), pp. 55–68.

UNCTAD (1998) *World Investment Report: Trends and Determinants,* Geneva: UN.

Vernon, R. (1971) *Sovereignty at Bay*, New York: Basic Books.

Welsh Affairs Committee (1988) *Inward Investment into Wales and its Interaction with Regional and EEC Policies,* London: HMSO.

Welsh Office, *Welsh Economic Trends*, HMSO, Cardiff: various years.

Welsh Office *Digest of Welsh Statistics* HMSO, Cardiff: various years.

5 Small Firms in Wales

Jane Bryan

INTRODUCTION

Studies of small business have gathered momentum since the Committee of Inquiry on Small Firms chaired by J. Bolton (1971) was appointed over thirty years ago, itself prompted by an extremely difficult period for businesses, and particularly small businesses. At the time, the subject was poorly researched and documented, resulting in policy based on inadequate information. Two things hampered this study and continue to do so: there are a lot of small firms, and they are very heterogeneous. In the absence of exhaustive documentation, the Committee quickly generated new sources. Chambers of commerce, government departments, banks, universities and trade associations were invited to participate. Advertisements were placed in the press resulting in 400 returned submissions. 16 000 small businesses were surveyed and a consultancy unit was launched working under a director of research, which produced 18 reports. The committee also travelled to Canada, Germany and Japan to learn about these countries' small firms. No greater *cooperative research effort* has been known since.

Published in 1971, the Report acknowledged the importance of small firms of which there were 1.25 million employing 6 million people, or 25 per cent of the employed population, responsible for 20 per cent of GNP. The Report studied in detail some 820 000 small firms employing 4.5 million people and producing 14 per cent of the GNP. Moreover, it found that the actual number of small businesses in the UK was smaller than in any other comparable country (Dewhurst, 1996)

The Committee concluded that 'the small firm plays a vital role in the preservation of a competitive private enterprise system', that it was 'an essential medium through which dynamic change in the form of new entrants to business can permeate the economy' and that without this dynamic small firm sector the economy would 'slowly ossify and decay' (Bolton, 1971). Hence, the Report switched on a light enjoining other investigators to follow. Indeed, with so many carrying torches today, it is remarkable that there is still little true consensus on which policies are effective, why some regions do well and others flounder, and which small businesses should be marked out for favour, if any. There is no doubt, however, that small firms will continue to excite attention and challenge policy-makers, because they are prolific and their diversity is perhaps as rich as human nature itself. The proposition here is that Wales' traditions and economic trajectory have modified how small businesses are perceived by both policy-makers and would-be entrepreneurs, and that alterations to this are required to ensure future success.

The next section of this chapter provides a back-drop for the discussion and concludes that the UK political environment has consistently sought to recognise the potential economic value of small firms. The third section suggests that Wales has followed a development policy designed to deliver high-profile results. The following section examines small firms in Wales and finds that Wales is one of the poorest performers in respect of start-up rates and sales per employee. The fifth and sixth sections explore the difficulties in developing realistic policy and realistic expectations from small firms themselves. The seventh section suggests some key issues in the development of new strategy for small firms, while conclusions are drawn in the final section.

THE POLITICAL BACKGROUND

The political environment holds a key position in both shaping interpretations of the role of small business and those policies designed to assist the sector. With newly-vested local autonomy in Wales through devolution, and as more English regions seek their own self-determination, regional politics can have a decisive role in influencing the nature and level of economic contribution made by small firms.

The Bolton Report was a political response to hardships faced by small businesses in the late 1960s, and its greatest achievement was perhaps to provide the first measure of the inconspicuous economic effort of many of the working population of Great Britain. Subsequently, Margaret Thatcher's Conservative government continued to raise small businesses to prominence. In the UK, free market thinking has always been implicit; yielding a society whose individuals have unrestricted access to, and power to dispose of, the factors of production (Goss, 1991). Small firms form the bulk of stock of competing suppliers who jostle to fulfil consumer demand in an entrepreneurial 'enterprise' culture. Pro-Thatcherites have argued that nationalisation, local authorities and trade unionism has been responsible for both the preservation of inefficient industrial practices and the weakening of the small business sector; with the result that the UK small business sector is less vigorous than those of her major international competitors.

Meanwhile, Marxists have argued that small manufacturing businesses are a 'moribund' relic of the last century. But since such small businesses are persistent and not moribund, there has had to be some revisionist thinking. Hence, this persistence has been attributed to the functional relationships that exist between small and large business in the producer chain. By sub-contracting out, goods and services are provided to the core sector more cheaply and flexibly. The small firm, under this controversial paradigm, is then an extension of a large firms' production function, necessary more for the latter's survival prospects than the former, to which risk has been transferred. In the 1980s, British Steel in Wales off-loaded slag reduction and steel transportation across site to sub-contractors in precisely this manner (Bryan *et al.*, 1994). Other examples of supplier relationships abound and are well-documented, (Thoburn and Takashima, 1992; Curran and Blackburn, 1994). There still remains much controversy regarding who benefits most from tight supply-chain relationships.

Up to the late 1970s, contemporary thinking emphasised the evolution in industrial economies towards domination of large organisations (World Bank, 1978; De Vries, 1979) to the extent that countries with large numbers of small firms were regarded as industrially backward (Anderson, 1982; Schmitz, 1982). Hence, there may be some ambivalence regarding the appropriate role of the small firm in society.

In the UK, high unemployment and structural changes were important factors in the increase in self-employment during the 1980s and 1990s, which grew to 13 per cent of the working population from 8 per cent through the 1970s (ONS, *Regional Trends*, various). The 1980s was also a decade characterised by government economic policy favouring entrepreneurial activity, and taxes were cut to increase incentives. The highest rate of income tax fell from 83 per cent to 40 per cent between 1979 and 1988. Corporation tax fell from 53 per cent to 35 per cent and the small companies rate was reduced from 42 per cent to 25 per cent. Small companies were allowed to make one VAT return a year, and they were exempted from certain requirements relating to industrial tribunals, unfair dismissal and maternity reinstatement. In 1994 the audit requirements for small firms were reduced. The government encouraged banks to make loan finance available, and stimulated the growth of the venture capital industry. Between 1983 and 1993 the

Business Expansion Scheme enabled investors to put money into a business and take any profit made free of tax. The Loan Guarantee Scheme was introduced in 1981: a measure of its 'success' led to the claim by many small firms, bankrupted during the 1990s recession, that banks had lent too much too freely. In 1988 the Department of Trade and Industry launched the Enterprise Initiative which offered subsidised training and consultancy for small businesses in areas such as marketing, new technology and production. Training and Enterprise Councils (TECs) and Local Enterprise Agencies were launched to execute the initiative. The Enterprise Allowance Scheme encouraged the unemployed to set up on their own: participants were given help to produce a training plan and £40 a week for a year to help them establish their own business. Indeed, between its start in 1983 and April 1991, 500 000 people participated in the UK (Anderton, 1995).

Following the 1997 elections delivering New Labour to power, and promising devolution to Wales, there has been little sign of any real departure from the free enterprise mores that preceded. Indeed, the evident courtship of middle England seems set to continue, with no immediate *volte face* in respect of small firm policy. One of the principal thrusts of the March 1999 budget was assisting entrepreneurs and small businesses. The small companies rate (SCR) of corporation tax fell to 20 per cent on 1 April 1999, and a 10 per cent rate applying to taxable profits of up to £10 000 was introduced. New enterprise management incentives were introduced to provide tax relief for certain forms of equity-based remuneration in an attempt to raise the management calibre in small high-risk trading companies. Proposals were also set out for a research and development tax credit for small firms based on the costs of their R&D expenditure. These latter measures will be legislated for in the Finance Bill 2000, (Peacheys, 1999). The message from New Labour with regard to the small firms sector is then sympathetic. Having said that, any government measures which increase the bureaucratic burden of businesses in general will undoubtedly be felt more resoundingly in small firms.

From this broad discussion two important points can be teased out. First, the political environment has accepted the persistence of small firms and, indeed, attempted to encourage the viability of small firm activity as a way of making an economic living, as well as its social credibility, through policy signals. Secondly, the discussion provokes the question of paradox. If small firms are quintessentially an expression of entrepreneurialism and individual self-determination, then what constitutes appropriate intervention? Moreover, given the profusion of small firms, and limitations imposed by scarce resources to assist them, what should be realistically expected from policy efforts?

IS WALES DIFFERENT?

There will be few strangers to Wales's industrial heritage, when coal and steel determined where cities grew, where roads and rails were laid, and how people were employed. Prior to the nationalisation of the coal industry in 1947, coal owners were externally-based and disengaged from Welsh economic life so that now, 'it was if they had never been' (Williams, 1990, quoted in Morgan, 1997). Later, the decline of coal and productivity gains in steel through massive capital expenditure programmes in the 1980s created an inexorable wave of unemployment. The economic imperative became one of finding alternative employment, and the challenge was to do it quickly and overtly. This was not a visionary or far-sighted approach. It was the speediest possible mitigation of a pressing and destructive decline. Indeed, even in 1998, *Pathway to Prosperity* described inward investment as 'the quickest acting (and the most visible) tool for shifting the balance of activity' (Welsh Office, 1998). Hence, policy efforts continue to turn to attracting visible projects where the winning denominator is employment. FDI manufacturing firms in Wales now employ over 75 000, over a third of the manufacturing workforce. Their role in maintaining the importance of the manufacturing sector has also been significant. Wales derived 33.7 per cent of her GDP (factor cost) from industry in 1995 compared with 29.2 per cent for the UK and 29.7 per cent for the EU15, (ONS, *Regional Trends*, 1998). While average firm sizes in the manufacturing sector tend to be larger than for other sectors, the average size of FDI firms in Wales is also higher (192 employees) than for the sector as a whole (40 employees), with the average for electronic/electrics higher still at just under 400 employees (Roberts, 1996).

Wales had a 14 per cent share of the 314 manufacturing direct inward investment projects won by the UK in 1996/7, compared to 1 per cent of the 178 non-manufacturing projects won. Meanwhile, 39 per cent of the non-manufacturing projects went to the south-east (or 46 per cent of all non-manufacturing projects in England). Dunning (1985) concluded that FDI had contributed to restructuring the UK economy. If the assertion is correct, it follows then that its impacts will have been felt most profoundly in areas where it is prevalent, as in Wales. Few would dispute that Wales' success in attracting inward investment is a function of agency effort and the direction of that effort. *Pathway to Prosperity* notes that

> Inward investment has been particularly concentrated in manufacturing, where it has helped to build sectoral strengths in automotive components, consumer and office electronics, aerospace and semiconducters. It has also helped demonstrate new techniques to the smaller supplier companies. (Welsh Office, 1998)

Regional Preferential Assistance is an integral part of the attraction and Wales has won increasing shares of a dwindling pot in the last decade, so that while the absolute spend in Wales has declined by 12%, this compares favourably to the 40 per cent drop overall in the UK since 1988. The purpose of this assistance is 'to create jobs in areas of high unemployment and to attract inward investment *into the UK*', and is awarded for 'the development or modernisation of *an industry*' if it is 'likely to provide, maintain or safeguard employment' (Trade and Industry Committee, Fourth Report, 1995).

SMALL FIRMS IN WALES

Low business birth-rates in Wales have been reported (Morgan and Morgan, 1998) and, indeed, Figure 5.1 shows that Wales' share of UK firm formation (all sectors) has fallen between 1985 and 1996. While deregistrations also fell off during the period, the net result was a 3.6

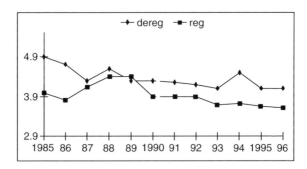

Figure 5.1 Registrations and deregistrations: Wales as a UK share, 1985–96
Source Small Firms Statistics Unit.

per cent reduction of stock in Wales up to 1997, during which time the UK as a whole experienced a 12 per cent increase in stock.

Figure 5.2 plots the production sector in Wales as a share of UK production stops and starts, and reveals a slightly different pattern. First, the production sector in Wales was clearly more volatile than the aggregate plotted earlier. The late 1980s boom was characterised by increasing UK shares of both registrations and deregistrations, with an overall stock gain. The early 1990s recession was marked by falling shares of stops and starts, showing a net loss of stock, while over the series as whole Wales experienced a 27 per cent increase in production stock compared to a 20 per cent gain in the UK. Post-1996 (which shows business starts on the point of intersection with a falling stop trend) trends will have been tempered by the relative regional effects of the economic slow-down at the end of this century.

Figure 5.3 plots business registrations per 10 000 of population (16 +years) from 1994 to 1997 for the regions. Wales lies at the bottom end of the rankings above the north-east with a registration rate of 27 per 10 000 population in 1997, compared to the UK average of 39. Some unitary authorities in Wales perform on or near the UK rate; for example, Monmouthshire (39), Denbighshire (39), Powys (41) and Pembrokeshire (38), while Rhondda (17), Blaenau (14) and Merthyr (19) are well below the UK average.

Figure 5.4 shows turnover per employee by size of business for Wales, the UK excluding London and the south-east and the UK total for the start of 1997. Clearly, the south-east is a high performance region but its influence alone on average figures cannot explain Wales' lower average turnover per employee. Wales only approaches the UK average in the 500+ size-band, while in all the other size-bands, Wales

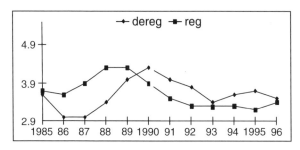

Figure 5.2 Production sector registrations and deregistrations: Wales as a UK share 1985 to 1996,
Source: Small Firms Statistics Unit.

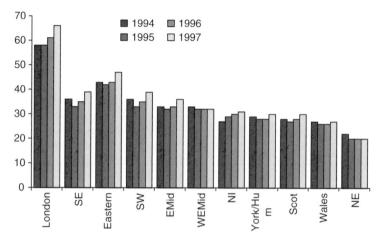

Figure 5.3 Enterprises registering for VAT by region per 10 000 population (16+yrs), 1994–97
Source: Derived from DTI, *SME Statistics for the UK*, 1998.

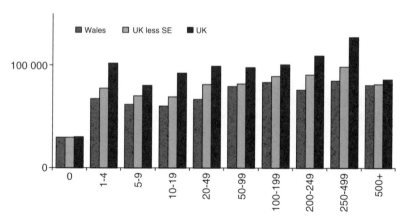

Figure 5.4 Turnover per employee Wales, UK (excluding the south-east) and all UK
Source: Derived from DTI, *SME Statistics for the UK*, 1998.

performs poorly compared to the rest of the UK. The small firm sector in Wales has below UK average levels of registration rates and below average turnover per employee. This constitutes a difference.

DEVELOPING REALISTIC EXPECTATIONS FROM SME POLICY

Given the strain on government resources, where economic development and industrial training must take second place to the hungry demands of health and education, it should be no surprise that initiatives have tended, in the past, to take place where they were likely to have highly visible successes. Meanwhile, analysis of aggregate data suggests two imperatives for Wales, with regard to small firms: first, the need to stimulate a greater number of enterprise starts and, secondly, to improve the productivity of the sector.

There has been an appreciable shift in emphasis in Wales today, as policy-makers turn their attentions increasingly to the Small and Medium-sized Enterprise (SME) sector. Government intelligence on small firms was generalised in *Pathway to Prosperity* (Welsh Office, 1998):

- They lack the capacity for training, management development, innovation or growth and so remain uncompetitive.
- They have an uncompetitive attitude towards growth and exporting.
- They attach little importance to information technology.

Pathway to Prosperity prescribes

> the establishment of a New Entrepreneurship Action Plan for Wales, which will be co-ordinated by the WDA with the aim of bringing together all the individuals and organisations contributing to the development of entrepreneurship in Wales – in both public and private sectors- and build a consensus on how best to develop a stronger entrepreneurial culture to produce a step change in entrepreneurial activity in Wales. (*Pathway to Prosperity*, 1998)

This represents a new awareness of both the economic potential of small firms and the many difficulties they appear to face. It is also ambitious and there are several hazards to be faced.

First, there is a danger that this shift will raise expectations among small firms beyond what can be realistically delivered. Certainly, the real cost of improving productivity in indigenous small firms and encouraging their proliferation may be higher than that of winning FDI. Secondly, the knowledge gap between what can be learned from aggregate data and the plethora of multidisciplinary empirical studies must hamper the framing of an effective response. SME literature is abundant but disconnected. Seldom are efforts synchronous or unambiguous. For example, studies have shown associations between high performance and management educational attainment, while others have found that growth-orientated SMEs do not possess more advanced skill structures than low-growth firms (Vaessen and Keeble, 1994). Still others present evidence that the small firm provides an important field of opportunity and advancement for individuals, whose absence of qualifications reduces their chance of comparable employment in activities requiring more formal qualifications (Merrett Cyriax Associates, 1971) Training is generalised to be poor in SMEs, yet there are also studies which show that firms experiencing a scarcity of certain highly skilled groups are not hampered since they generate the requisite skill-base in-house (Oakey and Cooper, 1989; Keeble and Bryson, 1993)

Hence, there is a danger in responding with inappropriate interventions based on generalisations, or on high-profile assertions. Heed should be taken of Storey's cautionary comment that 'public policies to promote the development and growth of small firms have been developed rather faster than our knowledge about small firms' (1990).

Thirdly, recall that a long history of national government interest and support for small firms has left Wales as it is. One could conclude that the wrong things have been done, or not enough, or perhaps even that enough is not a possibility. Given these difficulties, any policy intervention must be careful and honest in its message or it is destined to fail.

DEVELOPING REALISTIC EXPECTATIONS FROM SMEs

There are an estimated 154 000 firms in Wales, each employing less than 50 people (DTI, 1998). Over 90 per cent of these employ four people or less, just over 4 per cent of these firms are manufacturers. Of a total of 158 000 firms less than 50 per cent were registered for VAT; of those, 7.5 per cent were manufacturing firms. However, only a very small share of the total falls into the turnover range of £5m to £100m from which group one would expect some 10 per cent to have the potential to be fast growth 'gazelles', using the Ten Percenters criterion (initiated by Storey in 1992). The rest will grow much more slowly or not at all. Some will endure for many years, providing stable employment for a few in each firm while together providing a far greater employment impact. Half of the new firms registering at any time will not survive beyond three years. Many firms are wholesalers, retailers, farmers, builders and financial services on whom policy is perhaps less obviously focused. Meanwhile, the size and diversity of the sector necessarily means that any assistance will need to be rationed.

This implicit notion has led to a shopping bag into which the small firm can put training, IT, export support, business networks, supply chains, research and development, innovation and so on; all of which are easily grasped, tangible responses to potential small firm short-comings. They are apparently there for the delectation of all. Rather less sophisticated is the manner of distribution. Policy can be reactive or proactive, that is it can aim to seek out the potential high-flyers or it can supply assistance, grants and expertise to those who demand it. The system currently defaults to the latter, while agencies, quite correctly, ponder on how best to focus proactive mechanisms.

The findings of the annual *Ten Percenters Report* (Storey, ibid) are attractive to policy makers. The Report showed that winning small firms exploit niches thrown up by social, economic, technological or legislative change and exhibit a single-minded management preoccupa-tion with retaining the niche, once found, through a strong focus on their customer needs. Inception of these businesses was the product of entrepreneurial effort, and success owed more to the individual style and drive of the decision-maker within the firm, rather than to any magic policy prescription. These firms had winning in common, but any generalisation regarding their capacity to train, innovate, export or to support the locality would be spurious, for common rules are likely to be few. Arguably these canny 'gazelles' are in least need of interven-tion since they are winners anyway.

Small firms can also form part of the local producer supply chain and, indeed, small firms in Wales are often discussed in the context of their role as 'feeders' to inward investors. Morgan states that, 'ways to improve the business start-up rate and the rate of expansion of existing firms must be found... Since many firms are being encouraged to operate in co-operative networks, the place to start would seem to be the subcontracting system'. He also says of supplier groups in Wales that 'large inward investors have come to dominate these associations and in Wales the WDA has actively targeted these groups through the formation of supplier associations. ... the WDA promotes these agree-ments because of their role in spreading risks and reducing the costs associated with product development' (Morgan, 1998). Yet, propo-nents of policies which encourage vertical disintegration in certain sectors, such as electronics, must recall the past structural dependencies which made Wales vulnerable and contributed to her present exigencies. Strengthening local supply lines to inward investors, for example, has been a rational way of optimising the role of foreign firms but does not fully mitigate the dangers of the implied dependency.

The best small firms are very good indeed at what they do, though not necessarily in how they do it. Other small firms may be quite sophisticated in their managerial approach but still fail to qualify as winners. Local sub-contract firms do not need to be good at exporting and probably their growth path will be determined principally by their local customers. Exporters are probably 'specialists', for the more a firm specialises the less likely it is that the local market will provide sufficient demand for its output (Curran and Blackburn, 1994). The fastest growing firms, the so-called 'ten per centers' may well be poor engines of employment growth in the short-term, and indeed an economy cannot pin its hopes on so few. Furthermore, interventions which encourage employment (input) growth will not necessarily be highly correlated with output growth. Wray (1998) has voiced the concern that grant structures which are biased towards the needs of short-term employment creation may alter the actions of small firms, by forcing them to make decisions that are detrimental to their long-run prospects.

Policy interventions which attempt to tinker with the internal dynamics of small firms will be destined to fail since only a few can be reached, yet, paradoxically, there must be understanding that many growth constraints originate internally. Hence, there are serious limitations as to what can be realistically achieved both from assistance to small firms and in how well they respond.

DEVELOPING A NEW STRATEGY FOR SMALL FIRMS

Wales needs more small firms, and better small firms. These are two separate challenges with separate solutions. In the first place, an economy cannot create a spirit of entrepreneurship overnight, since its essence is distilled initially within the social unit of the family and the community. Sons tend to follow fathers and operate within pre-formed horizons. A cultural sea-change in Wales must embody and communicate the message, starting in schools and within the community, that enterprise has special requirements: self-reliance, independence, courage and discipline. This message cannot come from politicians or their army of public servants; the 'thinkers' and 'wanters'. It carries most weight if it comes instead from those that 'are' and 'do' – the entrepre-neurs themselves. The New Entrepreneurial Action Plan will be at its most effective if it fully engages the small business community to breed from itself, and this will take time.

Improving existing firms is a different matter. Assistance is a finite resource, subject to rationing. It is, in a sense, a luxury item. Every award has an opportunity cost. Small business support should reflect both the hardships latent in self-determination, and the limits of the resource itself, and be hard fought for. Dewhurst suggests that *'perhaps we still tend to "feather-bed" start-ups, to encourage new businesses with financial support in the early months which subtly deprives the entrepre-neur of the need to fight hard for survival in a hostile business environ-ment'* (Dewhurst, 1996).

As a corollary, a discriminating financial support system should reflect the quality of battle, and reward the winners with much more than the derisory short-termism that is characteristic of the modern lending bank in the UK. The higher regard with which small business is held on the continent is reflected in the behaviour of its institutions. For example, it is not unusual for continental banks to take an equity stake in a business, while this is rare here. In general, there is a high reliance on bank overdrafts in the UK, where the decision process is more dependent on head office rules and regulations rather than any personal judgement on the part of the bank manager. This impersonality is unusual on the continent. There exists a serious mis-match between government policy encouraging start-ups and the attendant high-risk nature of the process on the one hand, and the security-conscious low-risk behaviour of the banking community. It is hoped that the Assembly will deliver a frontier-breaking Small Business Bank to Wales, opera-ting a rigorous selection process and in return offering long-term debt and equity support, based on the development of matched trust and confidence; that is, hard-won and high-quality support.

There exists a circular dilemma of low economic growth rates and low levels of income inhibiting the expansion of small firms based on local markets, and technical impediments in the periphery contributing to lower product and process innovation rates. This is perhaps best broken by shifting the policy emphasis from job-creation to capital investment, despite the apparent conflict, as capital replaces labour. It is probably no accident that the most productive firms operate in the most inten-sively competitive environments. London, for example, is characterised by high levels of churning. Low start-up numbers in Wales are coupled with lower numbers of stops. A more entrepreneurial and competitive

Wales must expect higher failure rates as part of the drive towards excellence.

Managerial and skilled labour supply bottlenecks exist in Wales, but identifying and inventorising where these shortages currently exist is again reactive. Storey makes no claim that all his 'ten per centers' can promise sustained growth, since many depend on scale diseconomies for their very existence. Some of these small firms are, however, operating at the forefront of new sectors where scale economies are feasible. These are the businesses, the very few, who will grow, and their skills needs should be served.

CONCLUSIONS

'We cannot wait for great visions from great people, for they are in short supply at the end of history. It is up to us to light our own small fires in the darkness' (Handy, 1994).

As with any critical analysis, this chapter has dwelled long on what are considered to be negative aspects of current policy, while only fleetingly visiting the alternatives. The purpose is to stimulate a new realism rather than categorically define a strategy – that fortunately is for others. The thesis put forward here can be summarised as follows:

- There has been a long history of support for small firms based on the understanding that they are persistent. The message in Wales has been diluted by its historical traditions and subsequent policy trajectory. The need for jobs has dominated policy for two decades and done more to reinforce the notion of employment in Wales but rather less to stimulate the concept of entrepreneurship.
- Recently, there has been a discernible policy shift which has occurred in response to increasing recognition of small firms as an economic resource, but Wales needs a bigger seed bed from which to produce winners, who will probably be few.
- Policy-makers and small firms alike must adopt realistic expectations of each other. Small firms do not provide the route to quick-fix solutions; they are too many and too diverse. Only a few of tomorrow's large firms will have started small; they will be in new high-technology sectors, barely imagined today. A few will be in Wales.

It may be a long time before Wales develops entrepreneurial vigour, for the spirit of enterprise comes from within and starts with fathers teaching their sons and daughters. It is up to us to light our own small fires in the darkness.

References

Anderson, D. (1982) 'Small Industry in Developing Countries: A Discussion of Issues', *World Development*, vol. 10, pp. 913–48.

Anderton, A. (1995) *Economics*, 2nd edn, Causeway Press.

Bolton, J. E. (1971) *Small Firms: Report of the Committee of Inquiry on Small Firms*, London: HMSO.

Bryan, J. Hill, S., Munday, M. and Roberts, A. (1994) *Steel in Wales: The Economic Impact of Steel Production in Industrial South Wales'*, Standing Conference on Regional Policy, July.

Curran, J. and Blackburn, R. (1994) *Small Firms and Local Economic Networks: The Death of the Local-Economy. London Paul Chapman.*

De Vries, B. A. (1979), 'Industrialisation and Employment: The Role of Small and Medium-Sized Manufacturing Firms', in Giersch (ed.), *International Economic Development and Resource Transfer*, Tubingen: Mohr, pp. 47–62

Department for Trade and Industry, *SME Statistics*, Government Statistical Service, London, various issues.

Dewhurst, J. (1996) 'The Entrepreneur' in P. Burns and J. Dewhurst (eds), *Small Business and Entrepreneurship*, 2nd edn, London: Macmillan, pp. 95, 107.

Dunning, J. H. (ed.) (1985) *Multinational Enterprises, Economic Restructuring and International Competitiveness*, Chichester: Wiley.

Goss, D. (1991) *Small Business and Society*, London: Routledge.

Handy, C. (1994) The Empty Raincoat, quoted by Paul Burns in 'The significance of Small Firms', *Small Business and Entrepreneurship*, Paul Burns and Jim Dewhurst (eds) 2nd edn, London: Macmillan Business.

Keeble, D. and Bryson, J. (1993) 'South Divide', Working Paper no. 29, Small Business Research Centre, University of Cambridge.

Lewis, J. R. and Williams, A. M. (1986), 'Productive Decentralisation or Indigenous Growth? Small Manufacturing Enterprises and Regional Development in Central Portugal', *Regional Studies*, vol. 21 (4), pp. 343–61.

Merrett Cyriax Associates (1971) *Dynamics of Small Firms*, Committee of Inquiry on Small Firms Research Report no. 12 London: HMSO.

Morgan, B. and Morgan, K. (1998) 'Economic Development in *The National Assembly Agenda: A Handbook for the First Four Years*, ed. J. Osmond, The Insitutute of Welsh Affairs

Morgan, B. (1998) 'Regional Issues in Inward Investment and Endogenous Growth', in S. Hill and B. Morgan (eds), *Inward Investment, Business Finance and Regional Development*, London: Macmillan, pp 23.

Morgan, K. (1997) 'The Learning Region: Institutions, Innovation and Regional Renewal', *Regional Studies*, vol. 31 (5), pp. 491–503.

Munday, M. (1990) *Japanese Manufacturing Investment in Wales*, Cardiff: University of Wales Press.

Oakey, R. P. and Cooper, S. Y. (1989) 'High Technology Industry, Agglomeration and the Potential for Peripherally Sited Small Firms', *Regional Studies*, vol. 23, pp. 347–60.

Office for National Statistics (ONS) (various years) *Regional Trends*, London: HMSO.

Peacheys (1999) 'The Budget', containing notes on the budget presented to Parliament on 9 March 1999, Peacheys.

Schmitz, H. (1982) 'Growth Constraints on Small-scale Manufacturing in Developing Counties: A Critical Review', *World Development*, vol. 10, pp. 429–50.

Storey, D., Keasey, K., Watson, R. and Wynarczyk, P. (1990) *The Performance of Small Firms*, London and New York: Routledge.

Storey, D. (1998) *The Ten Percenters. Fourth Report on Fast Growing SMEs in Great Britain*, London: Deloitte and Touche.

Thoburn, J. T. and Takashima, M. (1992) *Industrial Subcontracting in the UK and Japan*, Aldershot: Avebury.

Trade and Industry Committee (1995) *Regional Policy Fourth Report*, London: HMSO.

Vaessen, P. and Keeble, D. (1994), 'Growth Orientated SMEs in Unfavourable Regional Environments', *Regional Studies*, vol. 29 (6) pp. 489–505.

Welsh Office (1998) *Pathway to Prosperity: A New Economic Agenda for Wales*, Welsh Office Publications.

World Bank (1978) *Employment and Development of Small Enterprises*, Sector Policy Paper, Washington: World Bank.

Wray, F. (1998) 'An Examination into the Effects of Grant Aid on Businesses in Pembrokeshire', unpublished MBA dissertation, Pontypridd, University of Glamorgan.

6 Renewing Rural Wales

Gillian Bristow

INTRODUCTION

Rural Wales is currently experiencing a period of profound upheaval and structural change. The strategic policy framework being shaped is driving forward a new model of sustainable rural development, based upon making the best use of available resources to meet new social needs. At its heart, this model is seeking to transform agriculture away from a narrow role as producer of raw materials, to a 'multi-functional' role whereby it is capable of satisfying society's demands for quality food production, environmental stewardship and rural leisure activities. Simultaneously, however, the familiar pressures of agricultural restructuring, globalisation and modernisation continue to squeeze key elements of the rural economy. As a result, rural areas are having to strike a balance between a range of competing forces – dependency and sustainability, marginal agriculture and quality food production, community decline and regeneration, specialisation and diversification, global and local, 'top-down' and 'bottom-up', and competition and cooperation.

Whilst there is a much clearer sense of strategic policy direction emerging in rural Wales, a number of critical challenges remain. Not least of these surround the issue of how sustainable rural development objectives can be achieved given the conflicting pressures bearing down on rural areas and the constraints of a regulatory system which still renders small-scale agriculture and agri-food production marginal. The main types of economic activity emerging in rural Wales also need to be more clearly defined and their relationships with available resources better understood. Equally, there is a need to develop a better understanding of where rural Wales is now in relation to the goals of sustainable development, and to create more effective measures of assessing policy progress towards them. How, for example, can progress towards goals such as partnership and participation be assessed? And how do we measure the contribution which multi-functional agriculture can make to the rural economy?

RURAL WALES: THE DIVERSE CONTEXT

The problems facing rural Wales are well-known and documented (see, for example, the Welsh Office, 1999). Whilst agriculture continues to suffer long-term decline, it remains a major local employer supporting approximately 10 per cent of employment (directly and indirectly) in designated less-favoured areas (rural areas classified as disadvantaged or severely disadvantaged by the EU and eligible for hill farm subsidies). As the major land user in rural Wales it also plays a profound role in shaping the landscape and its biodiversity, and delivering wider social objectives. Relative to other regions, Welsh agriculture has not fared particularly well under the Common Agricultural Policy (CAP) which has promoted farm-scale enlargement, production expansion and a continual cost–price squeeze for small Welsh farms. Farm incomes in Wales have declined dramatically since 1996 following the BSE crisis, the appreciation of sterling and increased concentration and competition within retailer-dominated supply chains. The continuing depth of the crisis is illustrated by net farm income figures which indicate that in 1998/99, average hill farm incomes in Wales were £4700 (net farm income refers to income to the farmer for forming activities only). Furthermore, there were some 13 per cent fewer agricultural holdings in Wales in 1996 compared with 1977 owing to the accelerated process of farm amalgamation and decline under the CAP. This progressive decline reflects the continuing dependence of the small family-farm in Wales on a narrow range of livestock products, many of which face falling levels of demand. The decline in the relative price of these products has created an extremely high subsidy to output ratio, with subsidies accounting for over 100 per cent of hill farm incomes in Wales. This leaves many farmers extremely vulnerable to the protracted process of price support removal and equally uncertain as to appropriate future market strategies (see Banks and Bristow, 2000).

Rural Wales faces other difficulties. The rural economy is over-dependent on a small number of large employers, particularly in the public sector, and relies heavily upon low-paid seasonal and part-time employment in service industries. The capacity of local markets to support new businesses is limited by a small, dispersed population, poor public transport services and poor accessibility from urban areas. There are high levels of out-migration, particularly among younger and higher-skilled people. At the same time, in-migration (through retirement and lifestyle choices) raises the price of goods and services, particularly housing, and can mask the problems of excluded individuals and groups. These problems are exacerbated by the scarcity and inaccessibility of key services such as shops, schools, bus services, post offices and child care, coupled with high travel costs (West Wales European Centre, 1999). All of these problems contribute to the low levels of per capita GDP to be found in the predominantly rural unitary authorities of Wales (Midmore, 1999).

However, rural Wales does benefit from an attractive landscape and natural environment, a wealth of natural resources, and strong artistic and cultural traditions based upon the Welsh language. Opportunities exist for all of these assets to contribute to job creation in rural areas and the wider socio-economic development of rural communities. For example, the marketing of a large area of mid-Wales as 'Kite Country', since it is home to significant numbers of rare Red Kites, has succeeded in generating nearly £3 million of tourist spend each year (Welsh Office, 1999). Maximising these opportunities requires increased investment in the upgrading of relevant transport infrastructures, accommodation and catering facilities, as well as skilful marketing of the 'rural' tourism product (Strategic Marketing, 1998).

All of this suggests that policy responses to the problems of rural Wales must be integrated in ways which both match the range of internal and external pressures affecting rural areas, and support the various different economic, social and environmental aspects of sustainable rural development. These policy responses also need to be adaptable to the specific needs of different parts of rural Wales and their increasingly divergent responses to the pressures facing them. Areas within rural Wales can demonstrate quite different characteristics in terms of deprivation, new business formation, agricultural activity and migration (see Higgs and White, 1998). This places considerable pressure on rural governance to find ways to accommodate the distinct trends and capacities which exist across the different rural regions and communities within Wales (Marsden, 1998).

A NEW RURAL PARADIGM?

New Strategies and Structures

Rural policy and strategy has been under extensive review in Wales in recent years, following a number of new funding and institutional developments. This has resulted in both a high priority for the objective of sustainable development, and an opportunity to better coordinate policies for its delivery. The National Development Strategy, which was designed to steer development in Objective 1 and 2 areas of Wales, states that 'sustainability is the central concept that must shape the future of the Welsh economy' (Welsh Office, 1999, p. 15). In the single programming document for the Objective 1 area of west Wales and the valleys, the sustainability objective is defined more specifically as being,

> to combine a healthy well-managed environment with economic productivity and viability within a vibrant self-confident society, within which, individuals and communities can achieve their ambitions and express their cultural and social aspirations
>   (West Wales European Centre, 1999, p. 95)

The new Rural Partnership for Wales, an advisory body created in November 1998, has contributed to the debate by producing a Rural Strategic Statement for the National Assembly (Rural Partnership for Wales, 1999). This has, in turn, informed the new Rural Development Plan which has been developed to provide an integrated framework for promoting sustainable economic prosperity across the different regions of rural Wales (WDA, 1999).

These strategic initiatives are directed by the new National Assembly for Wales which has a statutory obligation to support sustainable development. As well as implementing and evaluating rural policies in line with sustainable development objectives, the Assembly must also adopt an integrated approach to decision-making. The development of the Assembly and the process of regional self-determination has also provided a powerful impetus to the restructuring of the rural policy framework in Wales. On the one hand, existing agencies such as the Welsh Development Agency (WDA), the Development Board for Rural Wales (DBRW) and the Training and Enterprise Councils (TECs) have been rationalised in order to minimise problems of service duplication and develop a more strategic all-Wales focus. On the other-hand, new cross-stake alliances between agencies have been formalised to enable support to be targeted more effectively at both cross-cutting policy objectives, and at different areas within Wales. For example, Figure 6.1 illustrates the strategic framework which has been designed for the delivery of the Food Strategy Action Plans for Wales. These Action Plans and delivery mechanisms were drawn up for the lamb and beef, dairy and organic sectors in Wales and were published in March 1999 (Agri-Food Partnership, 1999). The Action Plans aim to develop a vibrant agri-food sector through the branding of Welsh food, and by

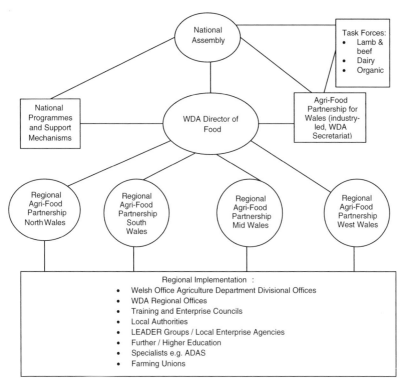

Figure 6.1 The agri-food partnership delivery mechanism
Source: Agri-Food Partnership (1999).

improving the marketing and development of niche products. They also aim to develop value-added food processing, to establish a network of demonstration farms to illustrate the best practice and to expand the organic sector to 10 per cent of Welsh agricultural production by the year 2005.

Additional objectives include the development of an all-Wales, farmer-owned, livestock cooperative for the red meat sector and the widespread improvement of R&D facilities for food product development. The Plans are being taken forward by the Agri-Food Partnership – an industry-led body working in partnership with the WDA – and regional agri-food partnerships which have been established for north, mid, south and west Wales. These partnerships are charged with implementing an agri-food plan tailored to each area's particular needs and for ensuring that existing local, 'bottom-up' actions such as *Cegin*

Cymru and *Carmarthenshire Farm Foods*, are better coordinated and linked to the strategic action plans coming from the 'top-down'. A similar approach is currently being applied to other sectors in the land-based economy including horticulture, speciality foods, alternative crops and woodlands.

New Rural Development versus the Old

The emergence of sustainable development objectives for rural Wales, coupled with new initiatives such as the Welsh Food Strategy and *Tir Gofal* (for whole-farm management), reflects the growth and success of new forms of farm-based and other rural development activities in Wales in recent years. There are many innovative examples which can be highlighted. *Tir Cymen*, the countryside stewardship scheme which *Tir Gofal* has replaced, has been a particular success story. The scheme ran from 1992 to 1997 in Swansea, Dinefwr and Meirionydd and offered annual payments to farmers following whole-farm management guidelines. A study by ADAS (1996) revealed that the average farm income of sample farms rose by £1600, whilst casual employment on these farms rose by 98 per cent. The ADAS survey also revealed that as a result of increased spending on both labour and materials by participating farmers, some 123 per cent of the value of *Tir Cymen* capital payments to farmers found its way directly into the local economy.

A more recent development is the rebirth of the traditional 'Farmers Market' in a number of areas in Wales including Carmarthen, and Devauden near Usk. These provide a facility for local food producers to sell their produce direct to consumers, with products typically ranging from high-quality speciality and organic foods, to more conventional meat and dairy produce. The markets are run on a cooperative basis with all stall-holders contributing funds to cover running costs. Whilst these markets are still in their infancy, there are a number of perceived benefits. Research indicates that customers spend an average of £8.80 on each visit to a Farmers Market (see the Soil Association website: *www.soilassociation.org*). Farmers benefit by taking home the market price and saving on transport costs, and consumers benefit from a more unique and personal shopping experience, as well as from the opportunity to gain greater assurance regarding the origin and quality of the food they buy.

Farmers in the Llyn Peninsula have adopted a slightly different approach to improving the return on their products, and have set up a registered company to market beef from farms in the area. All farmers involved in the company are members of the local producer group and follow its range of provenance, quality assurance and contractual specifications. With the help and cooperation of the local auctioneer, the local abattoir (*Cwmni Cig Arfon*) and a number of support agencies, the farmers have succeeded in winning valuable contracts for 'Extra Mature Welsh Beef', as well as supplying quality branded produce to local butchers and caterers. The success of the venture is perhaps best illustrated by the continuing expansion of the numbers of farmers involved and the emergence of similar schemes in other parts of Wales.

Many other examples of innovative action in rural Wales can be identified, from the expanding organic farm sector to the variety of local community initiatives such as telematics and farm trails supported by the LEADER groups, and the new National Botanic Garden of Wales (see, for example, Cardiff University, 1999; Midmore *et al.*, 1994). These cover a diverse range of activities and sectors but have certain characteristics in common. All are driven by a motivation to secure higher levels of value-added income and employment in rural communities by reorienting or renewing traditional activities to meet new consumer demands for, amongst other things, attractive landscapes, recreational and tourism opportunities and high-quality (often region-specific) food products. These activities are also characterised by a return to local, small-scale efforts, as well as new forms of cooperation and participation, and a common desire to break existing rural dependencies on public support.

The challenge of breaking free from dependency on the CAP represents one of the major obstacles ahead for rural Wales. There is widespread consensus about the need for radical CAP reform. Moreover, there is growing acceptance that the latest round of World Trade Organisation (WTO) negotiations and the prospective enlargement of the EU will place additional, perhaps intolerable, pressures on CAP expenditure. The Agenda 2000 package of CAP reforms agreed in March 1999 has made only tentative progress towards the desired reorientation of the CAP away from price support and towards environmental payments and broader rural policy measures (full details of the Agenda 2000 reform can be found at *http://www.maff. gov.uk*). Whilst the present system is failing to sustain agriculture in rural Wales, it is manifestly clear that waiting until 2004 for the next round of CAP reform to improve matters is not a viable option.

The new strategic policy statements for rural Wales make it clear that the concept of sustainable agriculture must lie at the heart of the future reshaping of the countryside. A sustainable agricultural industry is one that is

> able to support the income of the farm producer and his or her family, without compromising the quality of the environment, and in a manner capable of upholding the unique culture of the rural areas within which he or she resides.
>
> (National Development Strategy, 1999; see also UK Round Table on Sustainable Development, 1998)

The critical question then becomes, how will it be possible to guard against extreme changes in the structure of Welsh agriculture in the future, given the continuing constraints imposed by the CAP? More specifically, what can be done to protect family succession, to encourage new entrants to farming and to promote innovation on relatively small farm holdings? And what can be done to ensure that other, non-agricultural employment opportunities exist in rural localities for those wishing to leave the industry? In short, how can the innovative actions highlighted above become the rule, rather than the exception, in rural Wales?

PROGRESSING SUSTAINABILITY

Rural Wales cannot be renewed by simply reorganising governance structures or by policy-makers adopting the rhetoric of integrated and sustainable development. Rural Wales also needs the development of practical and innovative policy actions, better integration of sectoral policies in regional plans for rural areas, and the adoption of new targets and methods for evaluating progress towards stated rural development objectives.

Practical Actions

Sustainable Agriculture

Whilst significant progress has been made in establishing policies for the realisation of sustainable agriculture in Wales, there is much more to be done. Further scope exists for extending the *Tir Gofal* scheme which, because of budgetary constraints, currently only allows for whole-farm agreements with a total of 600 farmers in Wales. There is a need to explore how the scheme can be broadened so that the positive environmental management of farm habitats and landscape features can be linked with environmentally-friendly food labelling schemes and support for upgraded farm holidays.

Similarly, the network of demonstration farms being constructed under the new Food Strategy presents a further valuable opportunity. As part of the remit to disseminate best practice, this network of farms could adopt the principle of low-cost, low-input farming – or what the Dutch term 'farming economically' (Van der Ploeg and Van Dijk, 1995). This means producing similar levels of output as would be produced under conventional systems but with fewer resource inputs of energy, water and pesticides. It also requires that the financial costs of all external, purchased inputs be minimised. To promote the concept of farming economically will require support for farmers to change their investment patterns and production methods as well as the further development of 'short' food supply chains, whereby farmers are able to retain a higher share of the final value-added from food production. This requires that new ways be found of promoting entrepreneurialism amongst farm businesses, and that the lessons of successful examples of farm-based innovation be studied and disseminated. Much can also be done to improve the wider business support package available to farmers in Wales for R&D, management skills and training in the use of PCs and the internet.

The realisation of sustainable agriculture will also require that policy-makers in Wales become proactive in exploring the possibilities for modifying existing agricultural support policies, to better meet the needs of rural Wales. The Agenda 2000 reform of the CAP provides scope for commodity support payments to be tailored to suit member states under the so-called 'national envelope'. This will allow member states flexibility to compensate for regional differences in production practices and economic circumstances which might make restructuring difficult. There is also an option to modulate (that is, reduce) direct payments to individual farmers on the basis of farm size or production. A new rural development regulation has also been introduced, albeit with relatively limited funding. This has amalgamated a range of existing and new measures for rural development, including set-up aid for young farmers and the modulation of hill farm subsidies in favour of small farms.

These reforms have begun to establish the importance of decentralisation and flexibility as guiding principles in EU agricultural and rural policy design, in recognition of the diverse range of circumstances which exist across rural Europe. In rural Wales, the new rural development regulation is being integrated into the plans for Objective 1 and 2 programmes. Further scope also exists for rural Wales to benefit from the implementation of both the national envelope and modulation on a regional basis. The Agenda 2000 reforms have made some progress towards the 'regionalisation' of EU agricultural and rural policy. It remains for the National Assembly for Wales to further this process.

Support for Other Growth Sectors

Whilst the problems of the agriculture sector have to a large extent driven recent concerns over rural employment and prosperity in Wales, concentration on one sector alone will not be adequate to address these concerns. It is important to examine the wider employment opportunities in the rural economy, and to consider how best to convince more young people that they can find high quality employment in rural areas.

A number of studies have highlighted the opportunities which exist for rural areas to benefit from growth in activities which have both strong links with existing natural resource endowments, as well as the potential to reduce obstacles to economic development. These include 'green' tourism (that is, leisure and recreation activities based around enjoyment of the natural environment), arts and crafts, cultural industries, timber-processing, IT-based activities and the biotechnology sector (see, for example, Cardiff University, 1999; Welsh Economy Research Unit, 1998; Strategic Marketing, 1998). Developing this potential will require a much better understanding of the particular support requirements of these sectors, and the development of more subtle and solid support for their expansion. These studies have drawn attention to the low start-up rates for new businesses in non-farm sectors of the rural economy, and the particular difficulties they face in market penetration, product development and marketing. Midmore (1999) suggests that these difficulties can only be properly approached with better knowledge about the economic and cultural barriers which prevent indigenous small and medium-sized enterprises from both breaking into mainstream markets, and developing more effective inter-firm organisation. As well as introducing better marketing strategies and targeted start-up assistance for small rural enterprises, there is a need to explore the potential for establishing research-led clusters of 'green' technology firms around rural centres of innovation and sustainable development. These may provide a stimulus to the development of 'green' supply chains, linking industries based on natural resources to local firms engaged in value-added processing and, ultimately, to retail and tourist markets. More research is also needed to determine the potential for revitalised rural market towns to act as critical connectors in these supply chains.

Effective Rural Planning Policies and Processes

It will also be important that all policies affecting rural Wales, and not just agricultural policies, are integrated and tailored to better fit the needs of different rural communities. It is increasingly recognised that it is sectoral policies for housing, transport and rural services and so on, that determine the uneven development of rural areas (Marsden, 1998). However, these policies often contradict or duplicate one another and pull rural development in different directions. Rural spatial planning thus has a very important role to play in resolving the tensions within and between sectoral policies by integrating them at the point of implementation. The recent policy and institutional developments in rural Wales have already prompted a number of unitary local authorities (including Carmarthenshire, Wrexham and Monmouthshire) to re-examine their approach to rural development policy and planning. All are seeking to establish integrated rural development strategies and plans in recognition of the need to create both clear local frameworks for understanding rural issues and local contexts for action. These emerging local policy goals need to be formalised, extended and integrated more firmly into the new strategic planning framework for sustainable rural development in Wales.

The National Development Strategy has also acknowledged that creating effective connections between strategic, top-down policy-making and local, bottom-up initiative requires 'that people themselves are given the opportunity to be part of the building process, ensuring that the differing needs of the community are reflected in any regeneration plans' (Welsh Office, 1999, p. 25). Building effective processes for community participation and involvement in the rural development effort requires the full engagement of public, private and voluntary groups. The National Assembly must provide strong support for local tourism action plans, for example, as well as for the development of the wider concept of community planning, following the example set by

Scotland (Community Planning Working Group, 1998). The Assembly also needs to bring an end to the fragmented financial sponsorship of LEADER groups and the associated competitive culture of bidding for necessary funds. Effective policy leadership by the Assembly, supported by the coordinating framework of the Rural Partnership and the Agri-Food Partnerships, can do much to put all rural agencies on a more secure financial footing.

Targets, Indicators and the Evaluation of Policy Progress

The new policy framework will need to be strongly supported by sound knowledge about the likely impacts of the new model of sustainable rural development in Wales, and more effective measures of assessing progress towards its realisation. To justify extended support for 'farming economically', for example, will require further work in analysing the likely investment costs and potential economic and environmental benefits of these activities. As the West Wales European Centre notes (1999, p. 43), this is important 'so that informed decisions can be made as to which [sectors] are good bets for development'. This raises a number of challenges for researchers. A methodology must be devised to aggregate benefits from the micro-level to the macro-level, and the economic effects of constructed synergies between activities at the individual farm level and across groups of cooperating enterprises and supply chains must be quantified. Research currently underway as part of an EU-funded project into new forms of rural development will be important in shedding light on these issues. A research team from Cardiff University's Department of City and Regional Planning are involved in this research which will include case studies from Wales. The project is entitled 'The Socio-Economic Impact of Rural Development Policies: Realities and Potentials'.

Effective rural policy-making and delivery also demands better baseline information to benchmark future progress towards the goals of sustainable and integrated rural development. A number of gaps can be highlighted. There is an absence of reliable data on output, income, wages and earnings at the small-area level in Wales, and little or no indication of the rural cost of living. Limited information also exists at the local level to support judgements about the quality of life, social exclusion and deprivation, which are increasingly considered to be important indicators in providing a more complete assessment of rural development progress (see, for example, Higgs *et al.*, 1999; also MAFF, 1998).

The National Development Strategy (1999, p. 30) notes that

> the contribution of policies and programmes to sustainable develop-
> ment in Wales needs to be measured against specified targets which
> contribute to overall UK sustainability targets and indicators. There
> must be provision to ensure that sustainability is monitored and
> reported on to the National Assembly for Wales.

This requires not only the deployment of clearly defined quantitative
indicators and targets for development outcomes, such as numbers of
new jobs created, but also better assessment of policy and agency
progress towards delivery of *process*-oriented goals, such as
partnership, participation, decentralisation and the integration of sectoral policies (Marsden and Bristow, 2000). This represents a vital
challenge for rural research and policy evaluation in Wales, and
requires a much greater emphasis on supported self-evaluation methods and qualitative appraisal techniques (see, for example, Midmore *et
al.*, 1994).

CONCLUSION

As we enter the new millennium, there are positive signs to suggest that
a process of renewal is underway in rural Wales. The development of a
new strategic policy framework, coupled with stronger policy delivery
mechanisms and new initiatives in support of farm-based and other
forms of rural development, all indicate that significant potential exists
to revitalise the rural economy. Indeed, a new rural development paradigm is emerging. This is based upon a motivation to secure higher
levels of value-added income and employment in rural communities by
reorienting traditional activities to meet new consumer demands for
quality foods, attractive landscapes and diverse recreational activities.
It is increasingly being recognised that rural Wales is extremely well-
placed to benefit from these trends given the high quality of its natural
environment and its distinctive cultural diversity and traditions. The
task facing the National Assembly (supported by a strong research
agenda) is now one of overcoming the remaining constraints on sustainable rural development by pressing for further reform of the CAP
and maximising available opportunities for innovative and integrated
policy action. Only then can policy-makers build a truly distinctive and
sustainable rural Wales.

References:

ADAS (1996) *Socio-economic Assessments of Tir Cymen*, Bangor Countryside Council for Wales.

Agri-Food Partnership (1999) *Welsh Agri-Food Action Plans for the Lamb and Beef, Dairy and Organic Sectors*, an executive summary report, Agri-Food Partnership, March 1999.

Banks, J. and Bristow, G. (1999) 'Developing Quality in Agri-Food Supply Chains: A Welsh Perspective', *International Planning Studies*. Vol 4 No3, p. 317–332

Cardiff University (1999) *Rural Carmarthenshire Economic Study*, a report for Carmarthenshire County Council, the Welsh Development Agency and the West Wales Training and Enterprise Council, June, 1999.

Community Planning Working Group (1998) *Report of the Community Planning Group*, Edinburgh: Scottish Office.

Higgs, G. Hill, S., Roberts, A. and White, S. (1999) *Economic and Social Indicators for Wales*, a report for the Mid-Wales Partnership, North Wales Economic Forum and the South West Wales Economic Forum, June 1999.

Higgs, G. and White, S.D. (1998) 'A Comparison of Community Level Indices in Measuring Disadvantage in Wales', in G. Day and D. Thomas (eds), *Contemporary Wales*, vol. 10, pp. 127–170.

Ministry of Agriculture, Fishers and Food (1998) *Development of a Set of Indicators for Sustainable Agriculture in the United Kingdom: A Consultation Document*, 22 June 1998, London: MAFF.

Marsden, T., and Bristow, G. (2000) *Policies for Rural Scotland: A Method for Assessing Policies in Relation to Rural Development Objectives*, draft report, Edinburgh: Scottish Office.

Marsden, T. (1998) 'New Rural Territories: Regulating the Differentiated Rural Space', *Journal of Rural Studies*, vol. 14 (1), pp. 107–17.

Midmore, P. (1999) 'Rural Economic Development: An Agenda for the National Assembly', in, G. Day and D. Thomas (eds), *Contemporary Wales*, vol. 11, pp. 101–9.

Midmore, P., Ray, C. and Tregear, A. (1994) *An Evaluation of the South Pembrokeshire LEADER Project*, report prepared for SPARC, Aberystwyth: University of Wales, Department of Agricultural Sciences.

National Development Strategy for Wales (Welsh Office 1999) HMSO: Cardiff.

Objective 1 Single Programming Document for West Wales and the Valleys West Wales European Centre (1999) WWEC: Carmarthen

Rural Partnership for Wales (1999) *Rural Strategic Statement*, Report to the National Assembly for Wales.

Strategic Marketing (1998) *Rural Wales Labour Market Assessment*, report for the West Wales Training and Enterprise Council, April 1998.

UK Round Table on Sustainable Development (1998) *Aspects of Sustainable Agriculture and Rural Policy*, London, July 1998.

Van der Ploeg, J.D. and Van Dijk, G. (eds) (1995) *Beyond Modernisation: The Impact of Endogenous Rural Development*, Assen, the Netherlands: Van Gordum.

Welsh Development Agency (1999) *Rural Development Plan*, Cardiff: WDA.

Welsh Economy Research Unit (1998) *The Economic Impact of the Arts and Cultural Industries in Wales*, Cardiff, November 1998.

7 The Millennium Express

Jane Bryan

INTRODUCTION

How well goods and people move within and between localities is both a cause and effect of prosperity. Internationally, economists, environmentalists and politicians have yet to find consensus on, and balance between, the extent to which free-flowing movement impels an economy, its external (true) cost to the public and the economic cost of the impeded flow. This schism is likely to widen as pressures intensify for developed nations to manage their environment in a more sustainable manner, while less-developed nations also build still more roads, own still more cars, and perhaps abandon public transport, as they catch up. The developed world of the future is likely to pay a heavy price, in terms of freedom of movement, as it takes responsibility for the consequences of privilege.

The future can be described in the short term but can only be imagined in the long term. A very distant future, with an exhausted energy base and technology which has failed to provide sustainable alternatives to finite fossil fuel reserves, could see a return to a much simpler life where only basic needs can be met, where trade occurs only locally and food and warmth are paramount. But imagine a world of technology where movement can occur instantaneously at zero cost. Place would have no meaning beyond what it could offer the aesthetic senses, and borders would disappear since the notion of spatial competition would have disappeared. This may seem remote, but is not impossible.

Returning to the brink of the new century, where competition remains central, Wales sits not quite on the edge of a large and affluent Euro-economy, and much closer to London, itself the heart of the fifth largest economy in the world, the United Kingdom. The UK is a trading nation and over half of its goods are exported outside Europe, hence, its economic cycles in recent times have been allied to the global economy rather than to Europe alone. As the Euro-economy expands, Wales' relative position will move closer to its centre, spatially and economically, which means both opportunity and adversity.

It will not be sufficient to confine visions merely to how congested roads are or how unreliable rail is or even how to unite north and south Wales. Long-term issues are larger than this. Newly-devolved Wales must decide where the centre of its orbit lies, not only now but in the future, because this will determine its infrastructure needs, which themselves are important determinants of the future trajectory.

This chapter considers some of the possible outcomes of that decision process, in the light of current pressures from a number of quarters. First are the international pressures imposed on and by the advanced economies, which call for radical adjustments to current transport use. Secondly, a federal Europe, set on convergence within its expanding borders, faces the challenge of 'infrastructure catch-up' in its far reaches, while attempting to contain and rationalise developments in core regions. Finally, Wales, while it remains one of the poorest regions in the UK, will continue to depend on its block grant allocation, which is a limited resource. Wales' new autonomy will undoubtedly modify how much and where transport expenditure occurs, and of all the many claims on the annual budget, transport is perhaps the most vulnerable, given the current mood expressed in the government White Paper on transport dependency (DETR, 1998, A New Deal for Transport). The next section of this chapter provides a brief economic context for the ensuing discussion, followed by discussions of international, European and UK issues. We then assess, more comprehensively, the Welsh position, and in the final section some conclusions are drawn.

THE SOCIAL AND ECONOMIC ROLE OF TRANSPORT

There is a relationship between infrastructure, including transport assets, and economic growth. In the first place, growth increases the demand for infrastructure. Thereafter, investment in roads, bridges, rail-track, ports and telecommunications can facilitate further trade and wealth creation. New infrastructure then has important implications for future economic development. Transport also enables access to employment opportunities, social integration, social inclusion and choice. The difficulty lies in predicting the exact nature, extent and direction of the relationship.

Increases in wealth have tended to lead to greater car ownership and road use, and road transport has become predominant in the UK (see Figure 7.1). Evaluation methods for new road building in the UK have

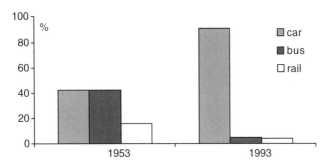

Figure 7.1 UK modes of transport, 1953 and 1993 (shares of passenger miles)
Source: Compiled from Department of Transport (1995).

traditionally depended on cost/benefit analysis (CBA) which compares the cost of schemes with the benefits derived by users, in terms of journey time savings, operating cost savings and accident cost savings, and expresses these in monetary terms (Department of Transport, 1981). It excludes quantitative considerations of the economic development benefits (or disbenefits) of a project to a locality and its neighbours, competition effects and the potential of a project to diminish regional inequalities (or exacerbate them). The UK government is increasingly predisposed to widening the evaluation criteria and does have the power to make discretionary decisions on these or other grounds.

Infrastructure is perceived to have a role to play in the redevelopment of depressed regions, which include areas with high levels of unemployment, low income per head, population out-migration, industrial dereliction, industries in decline and so on. Once the argument whether effort should be made to 'save' depressed areas has been resolved, a rational antidote is the provision of new opportunity, and infrastructure is a vital ingredient. This premise is supported by the importance given to the infrastructure provision within regions in literature published by development agencies and by the thrust of feasibility studies conducted by or on behalf of investors (Cole, 1987).

THE INTERNATIONAL MIND-SET

International transport thinking reflects mixed motives. On the one hand, advanced nations are increasingly intent upon rationalising movement, while on the other, less-developed parts of the world are seeking principally to extend their existing networks. Attempts to contain the environmental effects of the use of the combustion engine seldom appear to explicitly recognise the long-term implications of a determined catch-up process by less-advanced nations.

The case of China demonstrates the magnitude of the dilemma. Since the 1970s China has reported economic growth rates in excess of 9.5 per cent per year, as a result of its 'open door' policy which has increased the demand for infrastructure improvements (Ministry of Comunications, China, 1994). The fastest growth has occurred in the coastal provinces, where foreign direct investment has so far been concentrated. Meanwhile, more labour-intensive investments are gradually moving inland creating pressure to improve highway systems. Growth in output has also been associated with wage increases, which have had the effect of mobilising the population as people can afford to travel more.

The highway network in China totalled 1.028 million km in 1990, and yet ranked among the smallest in the world in per capita terms. Just under a third of China's villages still have no access to roads suitable for motor vehicles. Even so, over the last decade road traffic has increased by an average of 14.7 per cent each year, more than double the yearly increase in rail. In 1985 there were only 19 342 privately owned passenger vehicles. By 1990 this had grown by 477 per cent and the trend is set to continue (Ministry of Communications, China, 1994). Perhaps the one saving grace is that China has an opportunity to learn from developed nations who are now poised to re-embrace public transport, and is likely to finance new road building from road user charges.

International efforts to control emissions have been formalised since 1992 when, at the Rio Earth Summit, the United Nations Framework Convention on Climate Change (UNFCCC) was established with the objective of 'stabilisation of greenhouse gas [GHGs] concentrations in the atmosphere at a level that would prevent dangerous anthropogenic [manmade] interference' (information sourced from Japan Times Online *http://www.japantimes.cojp/cop3/main.html*). In 1997, representatives from over 160 countries gathered in Kyoto to review the earlier goals set in Rio, and found that cutting greenhouse gases to 1990 levels by 2000 was not achievable. The USA wanted to reduce them to 1990 levels by 2010, while the EU wanted a tougher goal of 15 per cent below 1990 by 2010. Most countries, including Japan, favoured more moderate objectives. The USA also proposed the use of emission trading permits, which would allow individual countries to trade the right to emit GHGs, strongly opposed by China and India. The Kyoto protocol recommended policies that countries should adopt to meet these goals, including research into new and renewable forms of energy, progressive reduction of market imperfections and fiscal incentives and so on. The main stumbling block of the treaty is its lack of detail and the fact that it is difficult to exact penalties for non-compliance. While the thrust of the initiative is clear, realisation will depend on commitment, which is tenuous.

TRANSPORT STRATEGY IN EUROPE AND THE UK

The same 'catch-up' dilemma faces an expanding Europe. One of the benefits of a euro-economy derives from the economic growth of new entrants who will then exhibit an increased propensity to consume. These trading ambitions cannot take place without adequate infra-structure. Necessarily, road-building and improvements are an integral part of the convergence process, embodied in the creation of a Trans-European Network (TEN): the European Commission envisages 15 000km of new and upgraded roads to peripheral regions in the long term. At the same time, there is certainly increasing emphasis on the movement of goods by rail with the intention that road transport will be reduced eventually to feeding major rail hubs (intermodalism) where possible. Germany and France are best placed to implement this policy shift, not only because of their spatial dominance of the con-tinent as transit nations, but also their rail networks have not suffered the neglect typical of the UK, and are hence better placed to absorb new demand. That these two nations also have strident voices in the euro-federal framework means that transport policy may well come to reflect their strengths, with the UK having to follow the lead.

It is taking the European Union a long time to produce an integrated transport strategy. The European Commission's 1992 White Paper set out the common objectives of creating an integrated transport system in terms of intermodality and network provision. Most recent Commis-sion White Papers have been concerned with the introduction of har-monised transport infrastructure charges over a ten-year period to 2004, taking place in three phases and resulting in a tariff system covering all transport modes. At present, there are nine rail tariff systems while five states impose tolls on motorways.

Given the current market structure of transport in the UK, where road transport alone remains under the government remit, setting out

an integrated transport strategy has never been more difficult. The
Government's White Paper on the Future of Transport describes '*a
consensus for radical change in policy*', and signals the introduction of
locally-derived and applied policies which are intended to improve
public transport and reduce car dependency (Department of the Environment, Transport and the Regions, 1998). New priorities will be
'*maintaining existing roads rather than building new ones*'. The White
Paper acknowledges the need for '*an efficient transport system to support a strong and prosperous economy*' and states '*we do not want to
restrict car ownership – with our vision for a prosperous Britain where
prosperity is shared by all, we expect more people to afford a car*'. On the
other hand, it claims that in the UK emissions from CO_2 from road
transport are the fastest growing contributor to climatic change and the
way we use cars carries a price for the economy, our health and the
environment. The Environment Act 1995, the Road Traffic Reduction
Act 1997 (which requires local authorities to prepare reports relating to
the levels of road traffic in their areas) and the White Paper (1998)
share a common goal of reducing overall emissions by 50 per cent on
1995 levels by 2005. Various measures are available to local authorities.
These are, for example, re-routing traffic around urban and residential
areas, restricting access, making car use more expensive or less convenient, and making public transport more attractive. '*"Carrot" measures are unlikely to have a significant impact on modal share unless they
are accompanied by "stick" measures that directly impinge on car use*'
(DETR, 1998).

Whilst the full implications of the European and UK transport
policies will emerge only slowly, several elements are already clear.
Integration and harmonisation will be sought at a European level
while in the UK much of the responsibility for reducing non-motorway
traffic will be delegated to regional development agencies (RDAs),
local authorities and devolved parliaments who will be empowered
through legislation to charge road users. National motorway tolling
is also inevitable. New road projects will occur infrequently or not at
all, with only those that are already in preparation or programmed
being built. While the government cannot restrict car ownership, it can
certainly impose fiscal and financial checks on car use.

Under this division of responsibility it will be hard for the public to
know who is to blame for the more unpopular and draconian measures
that are in the pipeline, and even harder for objections to be made
through the electoral system, which lends an inevitability to radical
changes to transport costs.

TRANSPORTING WALES INTO THE THIRD MILLENNIUM

While humans consume there will always be a need for the movement of goods. Beyond that lies the issue of the nature of consumption, which becomes ever more sophisticated and specialised. Economic growth depends on the creation of new products, ideas and activities on which increasing amounts of disposable income can be spent. There is considerable scope for rationalising movement in the electronic era, but even if a region is not producing intermediate or final goods, it will still be purchasing and distributing them for consumption. It matters little where manufacturing takes place in the global transport context, or whether regions specialise or generalise, since networks will always be required for distribution. If the UK and Wales were to lose all their manufacturing capacity, they would still be consumers making demands upon their transport networks.

The extreme scenario is one of a non-manufacturing, service-based society trading on electronic intelligence. Assuming the prescriptions within the White Paper survive several government terms, and where the end-game is one of sustainable movement, it is possible to envisage human life becoming more confined to tightly centralised cityscapes with occasional leisure skirmishes into the countryside. People would live and work from home, agents would operate highly rationalised delivery schedules from electronically received orders between distribution point and domicile. Travel intra-city would occur for social rather than business purposes, on solar-powered light rail networks. The fossil fuel powered engine would be considered as dirty as cigarette smoking and equally abhorrent. Today, for example, living in the country and working in cities is only possible in the UK because it is affordable, and would not be viable under draconian road cost adjustments. What does all this mean for Wales?

Much has been published on Wales' existing and planned infrastructure, including official government literature (*Driving Wales Forward*, Welsh Office, 1998) and the strategies of various lobby groups (CBI, 1996; Campaign for the Protection of Rural Wales, 1994; Transport in the National Assembly for Wales Agenda, Institute of Welsh Affairs, 1999). In the short term Wales knows what it will get and interest groups within Wales know what they would like.

Wales' transport infrastructure, as with Europe and elsewhere, has until recently reflected past activity rather than that of the future. Internal rail networks were laid principally to carry heavy raw materials and finished products between coal and steel yards. Wales' road network has been considerably strengthened in the last few decades under previous 'predict and provide' regimes, increasingly echoing the needs of current restructured activities. Wales now has two east–west TEN routes with improvements to the third, the A465, in preparation. The dualling of the A55 expressway across Anglesey will complete the TEN route to Eire, while extension of the M4 westwards is still under consideration as is the M4 Newport Relief road. No new major road schemes will be countenanced with the mood of the current government. Improvements of existing schemes are likely to receive greater focus, including works which reduce travel times between north and south Wales (Institute of Welsh Affairs, 1999). The road network in Wales is likely to change little from now, regardless of trading patterns. What will change is how the network is used.

Two factors combine to make road congestion a medium-term certainty in Wales. These are the termination of the 'predict and provide' regime, and Wales' ambitions to catch up economically with the rest of the UK, given the positive relationship between prosperity (economic growth) and road use. Traffic on grid-locked roads will result in increased GHG emissions, and delays will increase business costs. Indeed, congestion elsewhere in the UK has serious implications for Wales' competitiveness nationally and internationally, and was estimated to have cost the UK economy £15bn in 1995 (CBI).

Moving Goods

For simplicity, transport can be divided into goods and people movements. Freight movements are generated by manufacturers and the distributive trades. As a relatively under-priced but highly-efficient resource, the road network has allowed rapid growth of the road haulage industry and contributed to the prevalence of the Just-in Time phenomenon, where manufacturing companies have increasingly sought to reduce costs by lowering stock levels. Over the last 25 years there has been a 25 per cent increase in goods lifted (by weight) but a doubling of goods transported (number of journeys), reflecting these changes in industry practices (Department of Transport, various). A shift from road to rail would require radical (and costly) logistical or location adjustments from manufacturers and their customers. Until those adjustments are made, road freight demand is likely to be price-inelastic, given the current pressure for firms to compete on time, as well as on price and quality. Hence, punitive fiscal charges on freight hauliers may provide a substantial revenue stream to government, but unless hypothecated to improve the alternatives, will do nothing to reduce road freight dependency. Increasing the share of transport to total costs has price-competition implications, which must be felt more severely in peripheral regions. Fuel surcharges, which are rising at a higher rate than inflation, are a topical example of this.

In the end, increases in road charges will force behavioural changes by producers and distributors which will be the same as those required to make the rail alternative time-effective. The point is that for a shift to occur at all, it has to make sense on the business balance sheet, and since rail lacks the efficiency of road, it must compete on price. It is hard to imagine how this can be achieved without government subsidy.

The South Wales Eurofreight Terminal represents a 'modest-cost' but small improvement to rail-switch prospects, the commercial success of which depends ultimately on its take-up. Demand, in turn, is dependent upon the condition and euro-compatibility of track leading from the terminal, and logistical adjustments on the part of potential customers and the rail freight hauliers. In order to operate a fully intermodal piggy-back system from south Wales to Europe, tunnels and bridges will require modification, or track lowered and gauge enhancements undertaken to give the required clearance for the larger continental-size containers. While the west coast mainline route (WCML) serving London, the west midlands, the north-west, south and central Scotland has been designated a priority project by RailTrack costing £300m, similar plans for Wales have not yet reached the survey stage. Pressure to achieve this and more should be a priority for the National Assembly.

Meanwhile, sensible businesses in Wales will already be reviewing the implications of ever-rising road user charges, and taking steps to lock into the increasingly sophisticated logistics services offered by hauliers, as well as seeking transport partnerships with other firms. This is a serious challenge and easier for some than others. For example, those Welsh companies who are part of a non-local supply chain may have little control over these decisions. Indeed, rising transport costs will alter relative costs of other factors of production, including land and labour, which may lead to the entrenchment of suppliers closer to their customers and eventually relocations from the peripheral regions.

The quality of infrastructure as an attraction for inward investment has already been noted. The above discussion also points to changing emphases on how regions are 'sold' to potential investors. Regions benefiting from, and selling on the basis of, superior rail freight provision will be winners in the future. The Assembly can play an important role in ensuring that Wales is not left behind in what will constitute a significant marketing shift.

Moving People

In a sense, the movement of goods has somehow become a problem for others since the costs and consequences are passed along imperceptibly, with the 'hit' on Wales, while certain, difficult to evaluate. However, individuals are self-accountable for their travel decisions, and the price paid in order to achieve them. That the transport White Paper focused largely on policies relating to individual travel, reflects the need to engage commitment from the electorate to make a 'sea-change' possible. Real success in reducing car dependency will depend on a collective acceptance of the 'stick' and 'carrot' principles described in the White Paper (DETR, 1998). However, financial pressures on private motorists are deeply unpopular, which perhaps accounts for the careful sequencing whereby local authority measures will slowly be introduced first and become commonplace prior to motorway charging.

Motorway tolling (an issue equally important to hauliers) has not been the subject of vigorous public debate, and several issues remain unclear. For example, if its objective is to raise revenue, then the smallest charge should be made to the most people, so as not to deter trips (which would reduce revenue), assuming that demand is more elastic for private motorists than for freight hauliers. If the objective is to reduce congestion, then charges would have to be varied according to the time of day. If, however, the objective is to reduce noise and pollutants, then charges should favour vehicles which are more environmentally friendly. Certainly research has shown that hypothecated charges which finance the improvement of alternatives are better received than those which are perceived merely as taxation (Jones and Hervik, 1992). It is perhaps premature to expect government to make clear what its intentions might be, but it is a forthcoming debate in which Wales should participate, and particularly so given the advance experience of the diversionary effect of traffic through toll charges on the two Severn crossings.

In Wales, between 1994 and 1996, 90 per cent of the miles travelled per person per year were in a private road vehicle, compared to the UK average of 84 per cent and the London figure of 68 per cent. The Welsh people may be highly resistant to road charging for several reasons.

First, Wales is not wealthy. Raising motoring costs, such that roads are perceived to be a luxury for only the well-off to enjoy, may increase social division locally as well as nationally. One alternative would be to allot a minimum allocation of road time/distance based on some location index, with the option of purchasing extra units of time/distance, thus introducing a progressive element. Secondly, industrial restructuring in Wales and the strengthening of the service sector has created new and important opportunities for work and new car-dependent commuting patterns, but the balance between travel costs and income may be very marginal, more so than in other more prosperous regions which enjoy higher than UK-average incomes. Thirdly, public transport alternatives in Wales have yet to achieve the time and cost-efficiencies that are necessary to guarantee a 'pain-free' shift for travellers, partly because commuter growth from the Valleys to Cardiff, for example, has been rapid and has occurred during a period when road-dependency was not discouraged. Finally, Wales is a rural region, which requires special solutions and absolutions from measures which may be suitable elsewhere. For example, the degradation of village services here and in other more isolated UK regions, ironically a product of greater car ownership, has limited consumer choice in localities and increased the distance needed to travel to obtain services (Campaign for the Protection of Rural Wales, 1994).

Initiatives

There are initiatives, either in their embryonic stages, forthcoming, or well-advanced elsewhere, for which the public should prepare. Among these are car-sharing, more park-and-ride schemes, city parking charges and in the longer-term, home-working arrangements.

Car-Sharing

Car-sharing has obvious benefits for both the environment and scheme participants. Such schemes tend to be employment-based initiatives; for example, the larger firms in Cardiff such as NCM and WHCSA encourage employees to participate. However, current efforts to capture commuters who do not work for large organisations are less conspicuous. Experience from the USA suggests that residential-based schemes can work equally well, especially in rural areas (Hartgen and Bullard, 1992). There is scope, then, for local authorities and community groups to organise such schemes. Evidence from the USA also suggests that the most enduring schemes are those which are evaluated thoroughly on the basis of how many individuals participate, how long the 'pool' is maintained and the change in share of total trips. As road-user charges rise, there will also certainly be commercial opportunities to set up and run car-sharing, and the internet may be a useful tool in enabling this. Already, commercial organisations in the USA run internet sites for coordinating car-share programmes.

Local 'carrot' measures to encourage car-sharing by, for example, allocating a designated 'fast' lane to high occupancy vehicles (HOV) are well-established in the USA. Several stumbling blocks have arisen from such schemes, apart from the obvious paradox that HOV lanes only retain their incentive if other lanes are congested while having the overall purpose of reducing congestion. Negative behaviour such as using 'blow-up' passengers, car drivers recruiting passengers from among public transport users, and road-rage aggravated by others abusing the system reduce the efficacy of these schemes. The USA is currently experimenting with the idea of high-occupancy toll lanes (HOT) which allow single-occupant vehicle users to buy their way into high occupancy lanes by paying a toll (Orski, 1999 – further details are available at *http://www.itsonline.com/ko_hov2.html*).

Park and Ride

Park-and-ride schemes are likely to become an increasingly common-place method of reducing inner-city congestion. In the short term these will be popular because they could be considerably cheaper than inner-city parking, though less convenient. For the scheme-provider, the advantages are cheaper land costs and the subtle refamiliarisation of the user with public transport. Strategically placed parking sites on out-of-town shopping complexes could also allow multipurpose trips, combining business in the city with food shopping on the way home. In the longer term, park-and-ride could displace inner-city parking entirely.

Workplace Parking Charges

Charging car commuters for parking at their place of work is also becoming commonplace. The difficulty here is that, while revenue streams are being established, it is far from clear who ultimately benefits, and these measures are seen as punitive. One consequence of measures to increase parking costs should be a review of the feasibility of home-working.

Working from Home

In its review of telecommuting (working at home or an alternative location and communicating with the usual place of work using electronic or other means), the US Department of Transportation found that there were over 7 million telecommuters in 1993, representing an increase of 38 per cent since 1991. In 1950 only 17 per cent of US workers had information and service-related occupations, which had grown to over 50 per cent by 1980. Moreover, Rathbone (1992) estimated that 54 per cent of the total US labour force was engaged in occupations suitable for telecommuting. Among the 50 strategies contained in 'The Climate Change Action Plan' issued by the White House in 1993 was a goal of 1–2 per cent of the workforce telecommuting at least one day a week. In 1992 it was estimated that nearly 4m vehicle miles of travel were saved by 1.6 per cent of the workforce telecommuting.

While telecommuting may seem a desirable goal, certain preconditions have to be met for it to be viable. Telecommuters have to be able to work without supervision, have suitable home technology, a workplace which is free from distraction, be well-trained and in receipt of senior management support and telecommuters, and their supervisors must be willing participants. Telecommuting cannot be mandated for the above reasons, but much could be achieved if the public sector in Wales were to pilot telecommuting schemes.

CONCLUSIONS

The above discussion does not claim to be complete, for the issues are complex, unresolved and require radical re-evaluations of personal freedoms, the costs incurred to others by failing to re-evaluate and to individuals by doing so. There are also limits to the absolutions that Wales can claim because of its relative poverty. Welsh people can choose. As part of the UK and perhaps Europe, a position as progressive participants in the shift to sustainable transport can be taken, or the National Assembly can lobby and be lobbied for special consideration on the basis of peripherality and poverty. Future changes to how people move in Wales will not be without pain in the short term, whatever stance is taken, though long-term rewards may be high.

This chapter has explained the background to measures that may be taken by local authorities, the National Assembly, government and

Europe to reduce dependency on roads. It has also indicated initiatives in which individuals and businesses can participate in the process. Further, it paints a picture of a very different long-term future in order to stimulate thought and perhaps engage some collective conviction that the way people move from place to place now cannot be sustained.

References

Campaign for the Protection of Rural Wales (1994) *Wales Needs Transport not Traffic: A Critical Look at Current Transport Policies for Wales*, CPRW, Ty Gwyn, 31 High Street Welshpool, Powys SY21 7JP.

CBI Wales (1996) *A Transport Strategy for Wales*, Cadiff: CBI.

Cole, S. (1987) *Applied Transport Economics*, London: Kogan Page.

Department of Transport (1981) *Cost-Benefit Analysis Manual* (COBA), London: HMSO.

Department of Transport (1995 and various) *Transport Statistics for Great Britain*, London: HMSO.

Department of the Environment, Transport and the Regions (DETR) (1998) *A New Deal for Transport*, Government White Paper, London: HMSO.

Hartgen, D. T. and Bullard, K. (1992) 'What's Happened to Car-Pooling: 1980–1990 Trends in North Carolina', quoted in *Commuting Alternatives in the United States: Recent Trends and a Look to the Future*, US Department of Transportation, publication no. DOT-T-95-11 December 1994.

Institute of Welsh Affairs (1999) *Uniting the Nation: Improving the Cambrian Way: North–South Road Links in Wales, Full Report available from the Institute of Welsh Affairs, Ty Oldfield, Llantrisant Road, Llandaf, Cardiff CF5 2YQ, Tel. 01222 575511.*

Jones, P. and Hervik, A. (1992) 'Restraining Car Traffic in European Cities', *Transportation Research*, vol. 26A, no. 2 March.

Ministry of Communications, China (1994) *Summary Report of the Transport Seminar*, Beijing: Ministry of Communications, p. 47.

Office of National Statistics (ONS) (1998) *Regional Trends*, London: HMSO.

Rathbone, D. (1992) 'Telecommuting in the United States', *ITE Journal*, vol. 62.

Welsh Office (1998) *Driving Wales Forward*, Cardiff: Welsh Office, July.

8 Making the Most of it: Objective 1 Status, Assisted Area Status and the Valleys

David Brooksbank and David Pickernell

INTRODUCTION

The UK was among the first European countries to adopt an official regional policy as a means of reducing disparities in unemployment rates, with the 1934 Special Areas Act. Sixty years later regional policy is still in place to address issues of uneven regional incomes and growth. Wales has, for many years, had access to UK government schemes such as Regional Development Grants (RDGs) and Regional Selective Assistance (RSA), as well as EU funds. Partly as a result of these initiatives the Welsh economy has undergone a transformation from heavy dependence on the traditional industries of mining and steel to a more diverse economy. Policy initiatives undertaken by the Welsh Office, the Welsh Development Agency, local authorities and EU bodies have also helped Wales to become one of the most successful UK regions at attracting inward investment. They have not, however, arrested its decline in terms of relative GDP per head which declined from 87 per cent of the UK average in 1976 to 83 per cent in 1997, which is the lowest in Great Britain and only marginally above Northern Ireland (ONS, *Regional Trends*, various years).

This figure disguises marked differences between sub-regions within Wales. Whilst in 1993 South Glamorgan had per capita figures 11 per cent above the UK average, Mid-Glamorgan's figures were 38 per cent below average UK levels. The recently defined NUTS II area 'West Wales and the Valleys' has a GDP per head level under 73 per cent of the EU average. Along with 'Industrial South Wales', these areas are characterised by low income levels, high unemployment and poor long-term prospects. As such they have qualified for economic assistance of one type or another under both national and EU regimes.

The policies and financial resources that flow from these initiatives are designed to overcome the significant problems of these localities. It is therefore imperative that resultant funds are used effectively. Nowhere is this more important than in west Wales and the valleys, where the granting of Objective 1 status until the end of 2006 offers the opportunity for £1.3bn of EU funds, if matched with funds from the UK government and private sector, to help revitalise the economy.

In order to most effectively use grant-aid status, it is necessary both to evaluate the assistance scheme itself and the areas which have been given such status. This allows generation of policies which qualify for assistance and deal effectively with the problems of the assisted area. In this chapter we examine these issues. The next section briefly outlines the EU's policy towards defining areas for which assistance is available, followed by a summary of the problems which afflict the valleys areas of Wales now subject to Objective 1 status. We then identify the policy priorities necessary to deal with the valleys' problems under the EU designations of employability, adaptability, entrepreneurship and equal opportunities. Finally, conclusions are drawn concerning the task ahead both for those in the valleys and in Wales as a whole.

ASSISTANCE AREAS AND GRANTS IN WALES

Regional policy as practised by the UK government has become increasingly targeted at specifically designated areas (such as the assisted areas), through discretionary policies such as Regional Selective Assistance (RSA). This has also become the pattern in EU regional policy where Structural Funds, which provide financial assistance for schemes promoting economic regeneration, are specifically directed at areas where declining traditional industries have caused serious economic and social problems. Selected Welsh areas have access to the four types of EU structural funds:

- European Regional Development Fund (ERDF) which endeavours to reduce regional imbalances and assist disadvantaged regions;
- European Social Fund (ESF) which aims to improve employment opportunities in the EU through training;
- European Agricultural Guidance and Guarantee Fund (EAGGF) which assists in part financing national agricultural aid schemes and in developing and diversifying the Community's rural areas; and
- Financial Instrument for Fisheries Guidance (FIFG) which seeks to help restructure the fisheries sector.

In 1998 the European Commission announced proposals for wide-spread reform to the EU structural funds; the programme of support to the poorest regions of Europe. The funds currently amount to around euro 30bn a year. The new agreement was ratified at the Berlin summit on 9 March 1999 and covers the period 2000–06. It will affect all 15 EU member states and reflects the fact that the structural funds required modernising to improve their effectiveness and to better target the regions in most need.

The aim of these reforms was to ensure a fair and efficient distribution of structural fund support: some regions of the EU will gain, others will lose. The support will be provided under three new Objectives, which replace the previous seven:

- **Objective 1: assistance to the most deprived areas** In the United Kingdom, Merseyside will retain Objective 1 status, and will be joined by Cornwall, west Wales and the valleys and south Yorkshire. The Highlands and Islands of Scotland and northern Ireland have made considerable economic progress and no longer need Objective 1 support since their GDP has now risen well above the threshold, which remains 75 per cent of EU average GDP per head. However, both regions benefit from seven-year phase-out periods. Furthermore because of their particular circumstances they will still obtain funding for 2000–06 at least to a level they received for the period 1994–99.

- **Objective 2: assistance to areas facing industrial decline, rural areas, urban areas and areas facing a decline in the fishing industry** Under the previous Objective 2 regulations, the UK was a major beneficiary. However, with the proposed concentration of resources, fewer UK areas are likely to benefit in future. The total population coverage for Objective 2 in each member state is fixed according to a range of cross-EU benchmarks – unemployment is not the sole criterion for Objective 2 support. The UK government will decide which areas to propose for support, but this is expected to include areas of industrial decline, rural areas, urban areas and fishing industry areas. Although the UK will still be in receipt of about a quarter of the total Objective 2 budget for the whole of the EU in the period 2000–06, the implications of south Yorkshire, Cornwall and west Wales and the valleys being eligible for Objective 1 status are that about 3.5 million people will be taken out of the current population for Objective 2 funding, thereby releasing funds for other UK eligible areas.

Objective 3: assistance to education, training and employment   The new Objective 3, through the European Social Fund (ESF), targets problems such as social exclusion and low educational attainment. The UK will benefit from increased funding under the new Objective 3 which will be less prescriptive, with the needs of client groups taking precedence over those of the managing agencies. This reform will encourage local and regional initiatives and is designed to underpin employment action plans in which many stakeholders will be active partners. The reform means that the new ESF priorities should be highly congruent with current UK government policies and should be reflected in the national development strategies being developed throughout Wales.

THE PROBLEMS OF THE VALLEYS OBJECTIVE 1 AREA

The granting of Objective 1 status is an acknowledgement of the severe economic and social problems afflicting a region. The issues affecting rural west Wales are covered in Chapter 6, whilst the range of significant problems which trouble the industrial valleys are covered below.

The Valleys

Over the last two decades an increasingly visible split has developed between east Wales and the Objective 1 area 'West Wales and the Valleys'. The valleys, particularly the 'upper' valleys areas, have major problems in terms of inactivity and ill-health, which a relatively strong concentration in manufacturing and attraction of inward investment has not alleviated. Indeed, the valleys areas can be seen as deprived in terms of a wide range of socio-economic indicators, even compared with the rest of Wales.

In terms of skills and training, for example, there are proportionally half as many professional people living in the valleys as there are in the rest of Wales (that is, Wales minus the valleys areas). Further, only 4.7 per cent of people of working age in the valleys have a degree or higher compared to 11.5 per cent in the rest of Wales. Conversely, a third of all persons of working age in the valleys have no qualifications, compared with less than a quarter for the rest of Wales. The picture is not encouraging, especially given the area's consistently less-successful A-level and GCSE results compared with the rest of Wales (Welsh Office, 1999).

These problems are mirrored in relatively restricted employment opportunities. For example, 56 per cent of the valleys' working-age population is in manual occupations, whereas for the rest of Wales the equivalent figure is 42 per cent. There is also a higher unemployment rate (the valleys 8.1 per cent, the rest of Wales 5 per cent) and higher long-term unemployment rate (valleys 3.3 per cent, rest of Wales 2.3 per cent), especially for those under 25. Added to this, inactivity rates are extremely high in the valleys (see Chapter 1).

There is a relative concentration in manufacturing in the valleys (32 per cent of employees compared with 20.5 per cent in the rest of Wales). Whilst this sector continues to provide relatively well-paid employment for workers with traditional skills, this reliance may be a long-term weakness. Manufacturing in Wales is likely to be subject to increasing employment pressure over time, as in the rest of the UK. Meanwhile, few alternative employment opportunities exist in growth sectors such as financial and business services; where such employment does exist in Wales, it is not highly paid.

Finally, the valleys areas suffer a shortage of entrepreneurs. There is both a much lower proportion of self-employed workers in the valleys (9.2 per cent compared with 14.7 per cent in the rest of Wales) and much lower numbers of female self-employed (3.5 per cent of female workforce compared with 8.2 per cent for the rest of Wales). Consequently there are low numbers of small and medium enterprises (SMEs) per capita in the valleys coupled with low business formation and poor business survival rates.

All these factors contribute to the notion that the local economy cannot be sustained without continuing inflows of public subsidy. It is this attitude and its causes that Objective 1 status must address. However, before outlining specific policy responses, the strengths, weaknesses, opportunities and threats for the valleys need to be explored.

The valleys have many strengths to build upon. The workforce, with its sturdy community culture and networks can be viewed as an undeveloped resource. Additionally, relatively low pay levels can act as a catalyst to new investment, which could improve the long-term viability of the economy provided that such investment is not motivated solely by low wages (which would then tend to reinforce rather than alleviate the problem). Similarly, the concentration of manufacturing and in particular foreign-owned manufacturing may potentially provide benefits in terms of clustering, learning effects, supply chains and spin-off companies. Existing support schemes in the valleys are also useful building blocks for Objective 1-funded schemes.

However, if these strengths are to be built upon, then weaknesses must also be ameliorated. Persistently poor higher-order job opportunities, low education and skills levels, along with high long-term unemployment need to be mitigated, as does the propensity of the highly-skilled and educated to leave the area. The valleys infrastructure is weak in terms of transport and business units, and, additionally, high-quality development land is relatively scarce.

It is vital that policy-makers seize opportunities where they exist. A limited number of prime sites, such as in the Heads of the Valleys corridor, offer the possibility of attracting large-scale investors close to the constituent workforces. Private–public partnerships could provide quality support in terms of improved communications and general infrastructure, to create sites suitable for hi-tech manufacturing, science and service applications. The rich industrial heritage of the area also offers opportunities to develop cultural tourism. Furthermore, the potential for the higher (HE) and further education (FE) sectors to provide infrastructure and expertise, to stimulate an upgrade in education and training, is as yet largely unexplored. The next section outlines these policy priorities.

POLICY PRIORITIES: ENTREPRENEURSHIP, EMPLOYABILITY, ADAPTABILITY AND EQUAL OPPORTUNITY

Policy-makers face a sizeable challenge in optimising Objective 1. Recent reports, such as that of the Select Committee on Welsh Affairs, indicate that job-creation policies, at least in terms of structural funds post-2000, will focus on the creation and development of indigenous enterprises within micro-businesses, small to medium-sized firms and the voluntary sector. Resulting policy priorities are designated under the EU's 'four pillars' of entrepreneurship, employability, adaptability and equal opportunity, each then requiring the generation of specific policies.

Entrepreneurship

The prevailing culture in Wales is for the most academically gifted to seek employment in the public sector, academia or the professions, rather than in entrepreneurial activities. The development of an entrepreneurial culture requires a demand-driven, 'bottom-up' approach, drawing on the combined efforts and talents held within the community. Four factors restrict entrepreneurship in the valleys:

- the low social status of the entrepreneur, which is a particular problem within the south Wales valleys;
- the high risks associated with starting a small business, which are still perceived as greater than the rewards;
- the confusion that is often associated with finding the best support and advice in establishing a new venture is also a deterrent; and
- the problems associated with managing subsequent firm growth and development.

Efforts to establish a greater culture of entrepreneurship within the South Wales valleys should include:

- *Raising the profile of entrepreneurship at all levels of society in the South Wales valleys.* Programmes of enterprise awareness need to include all levels of education from primary to tertiary, as well as promotion of successful Welsh entrepreneurs as 'role models'. Measures to encourage self-employment (as well as business start-ups) may then have a higher probability of take-up.
- *Rolling programmes of enterprise support.* The concept of lifelong learning should also apply to the firm, and businesses should be encouraged to establish a continuous programme of improvement through accessing various business support measures.
- *Learning from good practice.* 'Cherry-picking' the best programmes via appropriate impact assessment (for example, Scottish Enterprise's Business Birthrate Strategy) and adapting them to the requirements of local firms should be promoted. Any specific initiatives towards entrepreneurship or enterprise support should also reflect this practice.
- *Utilising available academic expertise.* The FE and HE institutions of Wales need to be engaged in the whole process. Funding could potentially be made available, via the Objective 1 programme, to ensure that they take a more proactive role in supporting new entrepreneurs within the valleys, and that science and technology departments interact more closely with local technology-based firms.

Employability

Continuous improvement in workforce skills, particularly management development, is a priority. *As Pathway to Prosperity* (Welsh Office, 1998) suggests, the future of the Welsh economy (and its enterprises) lies in its human capital. Specific priorities include:

- *Creating a strategy for greater coherence between Wales' education and training providers.* Greater emphasis needs to be given to the needs of employers and the aspirations of the individual. A demand-driven, 'bottom-up' approach should be adopted for the provision of management-development support (which will be the basis of most actions in Objective 1), including the development of a learning strategy for all firms of 10 or more employees in the valleys, based on a detailed audit. This would identify the skills and training requirements of each firm, but would be best generated after a full review of existing industrial south Wales projects; some of which may be enhanced.
- *Developing an improvement in the management competencies of smaller firms.* The *Future Skills Wales* report (MORI, 1998) demonstrated that small firms require training in developing competencies in marketing, exporting, information technology, team-working, and especially understanding customers needs. Such skills training should come under the auspices of the higher and further education sectors, in cooperation with the Training and Enterprise Councils (TECs) and other relevant bodies.
- *Developing a range of measures to enhance small-business survival rates.* This should include funding for management development. As with all other business support services, it should ensure that products and delivery are matched to the needs of indigenous firms, rather than funding dictating the type of service offered. Facilitating a coordinated policy for management development in Wales and raising the profile of key business initiatives and targets are particular roles for the Welsh Office, Welsh Development Agency and Business Connect consortia. In addition, affirming the importance of national benchmarking and internationally recognised management qualifications will improve the ability of firms to survive.
- *Concentration on sustainable development.* There must be an overarching theme to the development of programmes that recognises the importance of sustainable, self-perpetuating development, which does not require ongoing government assistance. As such, support

for a (reorganised) Business Connect network must be put in place to ensure continuity of care in relation to improved employability.

Adaptability

It is vitally important that all firms develop their full wealth-creating and employment potential and thus help build prosperous communities. However, an adaptable economy requires a range of viable firms and industries that are capable of reacting to changing economic circumstances. Different types of firms and industries will require different types of aid. Whilst a full support programme for all businesses in the South Wales valleys will be required, it is also important that support mechanisms for 'growth' businesses differ from those for micro-firms, as their needs will be very different. Specific policy priorities include:

- *Identifying those firms with growth potential and fulfilling that potential.* Initiatives need to be developed which specifically address growth potential and identify existing strengths, through the development of network groups for valleys industries. As a first step the valleys' small and medium-sized enterprises (SMEs) which have growth potential need to be identified. The 'Fast Growth Fifty Network' (a network of Wales' most successful indigenous companies), established at the University of Glamorgan, might then be used as a template for developing firm networks within the valleys region. Alternatively, sectoral groups could be established in the South Wales valleys along the lines of those established for the Regional Technology Plan.
- *Linking tourism policy and projects explicitly to job-creation and local networks.* The potential of the valleys environment, cultural industries and community enterprise should be exploited in the creation of an adaptable economy.
- *Promoting purchase of locally-produced goods and services.* Agencies can do much to facilitate the 'embeddedness' of local firms by disseminating information.
- *Developing measures to support creation and expansion of the (export base/import substituting) service sector.* Such policies are important in diversifying the industrial and market base of the valleys economy and could include FE and HE initiatives to encourage graduates to establish local service-sector companies, as well as targeted inward investment.

- *Encouraging business investment.* Indigenous expansion and inward investment from the rest of the UK and abroad should be encouraged. Such inward investments form a major part of the current economic strategy for Wales. However, emphasis in the valleys needs to be placed on targeting and supporting high-quality projects involving higher-order functions and development or, at least, projects with the potential for such functions. As part of this, a full analysis of the efficacy of other regional development funds, such as Regional Selective Assistance spending in the South Wales valley areas (amount, types of industries, types of projects, nationality of companies, outcomes of spending and so on), should be made. If necessary, policy could be adjusted to reflect sustainable and adaptable development themes.
- *Providing clearer leadership and integrated delivery required of innovation and technology support/technology transfer.* It is vital to bridge the culture gap between firms, innovators and researchers. Encouraging graduate placement and employment programmes will be an important part of this process, as might also be exploration of the potential of the University for Industry to aid such development (Wales Labour Party, 1999).
- *Developing and linking supply chains and networks.* Existing supply chains and networks could be linked to business mentoring initiatives and the whole business development strategy, hence recognising the importance of the supply-chain links to inward investors and the importance of these continuing relationships to the community as a whole.
- *Capitalise on growth of high-tech/electronics/automotive/financial services in recent years.* Maintaining the momentum of inward investment projects into east Wales will be crucial, as will be spreading the resultant benefits of those projects north from the M4.
- *Build supply chains and infrastructure which recognise the pivotal role of the public sector.* The short-term importance of public expenditure in developing adaptable economies and communities should be acknowledged. For example, 'environmental goods and services' industries, such as recycling and reprocessing are to a great extent dependent on government regulation. Appropriate infrastructure for business development is a priority to be conducted at both community and regional levels. In particular, the development of appropriate sites and premises to meet the needs of start-up firms, growing firms and inward investors, including the M4 corridor and Heads of Valleys areas need to be in line with the themes of sustainable,

adaptable development. It is therefore crucial that sites have a mix of start-ups, inward investors and established firms, that they reflect the diversity of businesses requiring premises, and that they are able to support growth-oriented firms. This should include town-centre regeneration, retail renewal and regeneration of degraded sites and emphasise a larger proportion of office accommodation in work-shops, with appropriate high-quality access.

- *Development of appropriate support infrastructure.* This should include the services from the main utilities at certain development sites, including new housing developments, as well as telecommunications networks (Wales Information Society project), ensuring environmental consistency
- *Increasing the awareness and development of the community enterprise. Pathways to Prosperity* (Welsh Office, 1998) recognised the valuable contribution that local community-based initiatives make to the wider economy of Wales. The development of community businesses and local cooperatives has been crucial in providing jobs and generating wealth, as well as contributing to social well-being in the community. Less dependency by such 'third sector' organisations on competitive funds such as those provided by local authorities would be welcome. Instead, community enterprises should have access to funding on the same basis as SMEs. There also needs to be more formulation of equal partnerships with key local players, supported by training, mentoring and other practical measures such as childcare.

Equal Opportunities

A final priority must be to overcome gaps in enterprise in the valleys by encouraging female, ethnic and other minority sector entrepreneurship through specific programmes aimed at reducing the main barriers faced by these groups when developing a new business. These include lack of business and management experience, feelings of isolation, lack of credibility, limited access to finance and lack of role models. The following priorities are proposed:

- *Support and business development advice which does not devalue or denigrate what these groups are trying to achieve, even though they may be approaching it from different perspectives.* To this end, management training that is designed with these groups in mind must be provided, as should start-up incubator units. It is also necessary to foster contacts for business growth, providing networking facilities that enable these potential entrepreneurs to meet with contacts in large businesses and other SMEs who would be potential customers. Management training and mentoring schemes also need to be developed to encourage links between these entrepreneurs and firms with similar managers in large businesses. Encouraging larger SMEs to act as mentors could also develop individual management skills. On a practical level, provision of adequate childcare facilities would also encourage wider participation.

- *Increasing the linkages between education and industry.* Indigenous small and medium-sized enterprises need to develop better links with further and higher education. However, education providers must change their modes of delivery to meet the requirements of such firms. One example which could be adapted is the funding which has been made available in 1998–99 for the Further Education Funding Council for Wales, working in close collaboration with the TECs, to meet locally identified skill needs and to support training in key skills under the Action Plan for Manufacturing Training in Wales. Additionally, embedding the development of 'industrial villages' in the South Wales valleys into the local communities must involve both drawing substantially on the local workforce and creating strong links with the HE/FE sector in the locality.

- *A clear understanding of the type of involvement required.* It is vital to increase the efficiency of the business support sector through adopting a 'bottom-up' approach of all programmes to meet the direct needs of firms (and avoiding duplication of services) through a process of collaboration between providers. Related to this, it is necessary to ensure that the valleys are fully represented as a region on Business Connect (for example, a Business Connect consortium centred specifically on the South Wales valleys to enable support organisations to work together more closely and move away from a supply-driven target mentality). Future evaluative mechanisms should concentrate on measuring the benefits of any initiative to the participating organisation. Common programmes of business support (delivered by one or more providers) need to reflect the actual requirements of businesses in the locality and not be driven by either the needs of national organisations or local politics. Importantly, it is necessary to establish a common database of firms to be shared between all providers, rather than the current situation of fragmented databases that have very little in common. Shortage of data on the nature, quality, size and structure of the managerial pool in Wales also suggests a need for ongoing research utilising the expertise of universities.

- *Develop programmes that exploit the full potential of new technologies.* This is required to improve the effectiveness and efficiency of business, particularly in accessing new markets via media such as the Internet. Related to this is the need to establish an e-commerce strategy for valleys businesses in accordance with the needs analyses carried out by the Wales Information Society Project (1999). However, this must also involve developing the capabilities and competencies of valleys firms to utilise advanced technologies, particularly information and communication technology, to exploit the advantages of ecommerce. As part of the strategy approaches could be made to private sector organisations, such as BT, Microsoft, NTL and various computer manufacturers as partners in the development and implementation of the strategy

CONCLUSIONS

The granting of Objective 1 status for the valleys and west Wales is not a cause for celebration. Rather, Objective 1 status must be viewed as the catalyst through which the regeneration of these regions can be facilitated, with the obvious goal that at the end of the funding period the region no longer qualifies as an Objective 1 area.

The policies proposed require a high degree of cooperation between public and private bodies within Wales. This is vital if the goals are to be achieved. The advent of the Welsh Assembly must also provide leadership in this task, both through the allocation of funds and the hopefully inclusive, cooperative political process that the Assembly will foster. Individuals and groups from the private sector must be heavily involved in this process, not least to provide a balance with the more public sector orientated backgrounds of many of the members of the Assembly. Only through such cooperation and inclusivity can all the regions of Wales achieve the development that Wales needs to emerge as a dynamic economy in the next millennium.

Bibliography

Alden, J. and Boland, P. (1996) *Regional Development Perspectives: A European Perspective*, London: Jessica Kingsley (for Regional Studies Association).

Fast Growth Fifty Network organised by Dylan Jones-Evans in cooperation with NatWest, KPMG and Western Mail, Welsh Enterprise Institute, University of Glamorgan Business School, Pontypridd, CF37 1DZ.

MORI (1998) *Future Skills Wales*, report produced by MORI Research and Business Strategies for a partnership of organisations in Wales (available from only Welsh Training and Enterprise Council).

Office of National Statistics (ONS) (various years) *Regional Trends*, London: HMSO.

Wales Labour Party (1999) *Working Hard for Wales*, Labour's Election Manifesto for the National Assembly for Wales, 1 Cathedral Rd, Cardiff, CF1 9HA.

WDA (1996) *Regional Technology Plan*, Report on the operation of the RTP, a project managed by the Welsh Development Agency and the Cardiff Business School, Cardiff: WDA.

WDA (1999) *Wales Information Society Project*, Report sponsored by the Welsh Development Agency and the European Commission, Cardiff: WDA.

Welsh Office (1998) *Pathway to Prosperity: A New Economic Agenda for Wales*, Cardiff: HMSO.

Welsh Office (1999) Statistical Directorate 5, Welsh Office, Crown Buildings, Cathays Park, Cardiff, CF1 3NQ.

9 Innovative Wales

Meirion Thomas and Martin Rhisiart

The role of innovation as a driving force of economic well-being has become widely accepted not only in the UK but in mainland Europe and North America. The European Union has placed particular emphasis on innovation as a critical factor in its efforts to close the prosperity gap between the rich, 'core' regions of Europe (northern Germany, northern France, the 'low countries' and the south of England) and the 'less-favoured' peripheral regions of Europe (southern Europe, the Iberian Peninsula and the Celtic fringes) (European Commission, 1995, 1996). In late 1998, the UK government firmly endorsed the EU's emphasis on innovation in its own competitiveness White Paper, Our Competitive Future (DTI, 1998).

Wales has been at the vanguard of this effort to place innovation at the forefront of economic development thinking. The work of Cooke and Morgan (1998, 1991, 1990) in identifying the key elements in successful innovative regions along with the development of the *Regional Technology Plan* (RTP) in 1996 (WDA, 1996a) were instrumental in demonstrating the way in which regional economic development thinking could harness innovation as a driving force, at a UK and European level (Morgan and Nauwelaers, 1999).

Unfortunately, this position of relative leadership in innovation policy thinking has not always carried through into actual policy in Wales. Despite the existence of a wide consensus on innovation as an economic necessity, Welsh Office policies and programmes have rarely made the 'leaps' necessary to give effect to the expressed needs of the economy in innovation programmes. Part of the reason for this is the domination, until recently, of Welsh Office budget allocation by the UK Treasury and other central government departments – notably the Department of Trade and Industry (DTI) (funds were earmarked by central government for certain ends thus circumscribing the freedom of the Welsh Office to act). The National Assembly will be well-positioned to implement Welsh innovation solutions which will have received a Welsh consensus for action.

Reluctance to take a strong lead is not entirely to be laid at the door of government and civil servants; business leaders in both the public and private sectors have been slow to accept the importance of innovation. For example, early in the 1990s a meeting of economic development leaders from the public and private sectors and from academia was held in the Welsh Office. The agenda consisted of a proposal that Welsh institutions should adopt and promote an 'Innovation Tool-Kit' developed by a leading UK consultancy and being supported by the UK DTI. Those present now recall with embarrassment that the meeting, which lasted several hours, first failed to agree on a scope and definition of innovation and then failed to agree on joint adoption of the Tool–Kit.

The abortive Welsh Office meeting was an early example of the definitional and cultural issues that arise in discussions on 'innovation' and continue to affect the debate surrounding innovation and innovation policy in Wales. There are usually two dimensions to this problem. The first relates to the confusion between innovation and its more limited (but still important) relations, invention and technology.

If innovation is defined as the '*application of a new method or device*', then invention is the act of '*devising something new – ideas, machines etc.*' (Collins, 1997). The essential difference between these two concepts lies in the outcomes achieved – in the case of the invention, the outcome is the new or original item or activity itself; while with innovation the outcome is the 'successful exploitation' of the new idea. Placed in these terms, inventions are not necessarily innovative, and vice versa.

Similarly, the concept of 'technology' revolves around its definition as *the 'science of mechanical and industrial arts'* (Collins, 1997). In order to make either invention or technology wealth-creating forces, the introduction of innovation is required. Innovation is, therefore, the 'engine' which uses the 'fuel' of invention or technology to create wealth.

Confusion in dealing with these concepts often causes erroneous assessments to be made with respect to the extent of innovation within Wales and elsewhere. For example, discussions regarding innovation commonly fall back on the easier notions of invention and technology. Whereas technology and invention generally result in 'breakthrough innovation' which leads to the creation of concrete objects (products) or science (techniques) upon which measurement and analysis can take place, innovation cannot be successfully measured or identified with accuracy. It is generally an 'incremental' process rather than a breakthrough 'event', and one which comes into operation after invention or technology to create wealth.

It is notable that in dealing with innovation in Wales, the WDA has continued to use the term 'technology' in order to achieve the required strategic focus and funding for its innovation activities. Hence, Wales has a 'Regional Technology Plan' and the WDA has a 'Technology Transfer' department, in order to address innovation.

The second dimension to the problem of understanding innovation relates to the breadth of activity which its definition allows. Most importantly, the successful exploitation of new processes and techniques in management, training and even working practices can legitimately be regarded as innovation since they exploit new ideas, as opposed to technology, and give us a more generous view of innovation. This broader, 'softer' definition and understanding sometimes sits uneasily in an economic development culture that values square feet of factories built or acres of land reclaimed.

In attempting to answer the question, 'how innovative will Wales be in the next century', it is useful first to revisit Wales' industrial past. A common assumption in discourse on innovation with respect to the Welsh economy is that its industrial history militated against entrepreneurs and innovators. For example, it is generally understood that the heavy industries of coal, iron and steel did not provide easy opportunities for indigenous Welsh capitalists to flourish following the Industrial Revolution. With a few notable exceptions such as David Davies of Llandinam and D.A. Thomas, and later Lord Rhondda (Morgan, 1981, p. 66; Williams, 1985, p. 227), the innovators who successfully exploited the technologies and inventions upon which the Industrial Revolution in Wales was built had come from outside, bringing with them footloose investment capital (Williams, 1985, p. 182).

However, an argument can be made that the success of the Welsh industrial base was built upon natural innovators in the coal mines, iron foundries and steel mills, and that much of the innovative potential of the Welsh was exhausted in striving for safer, more efficient ways of working in dangerous, difficult conditions. Skilled workers made considerable innovative contributions, for example, at the iron works in Dowlais and Cyfarthfa (Williams, 1985, p. 184). Certainly any visitor today to the industrial 'themeparks' of the south Wales mining area or the north Wales slate quarries cannot fail to be impressed by the ingenuity and practicality of the small 'incremental' innovations that the workers in these places developed in order to make their work safer, easier and more productive. Simple devices such as door-opening mechanisms, lamp-testers and roadway brakes are all testament to the largely unacknowledged innovative capacity of Wales' industrial forefathers.

In the same way that Japanese industry has embraced the 'team-work' philosophy in order to sharpen worker commitment and utilise innovation skills born of practical experience (Funk, 1992), the coal miners, quarry workers, foundrymen and steel workers of the nine-teenth and early twentieth centuries were active innovators in their own right with little economic recognition for their contributions. They were not generally inventors or technologists, but may be regarded as the unsung innovator heroes of the Welsh industrial past.

Returning to the present, the *Regional Technology Plan*, developed over two years from 1994 to 1996, and revised in 1998 (WDA, 1996a, 1998), examined the position of innovation in Wales in a number of ways. First, it reviewed the statistical basis available, notably in terms of research and development activity. Second, it sought to refine the understanding of the nature of innovation in the context of the Welsh economy in the last decade of the twentieth century. The picture which emerged from the RTP process is one where the majority of companies did not view innovation as part of their long-term business strategy and indeed saw it as a short-term response to customer demand. These attitudes were reflected in the feeling amongst companies that innova-tion was unlikely to lead to substantial long-term rewards. Partly as a result of this, few companies considered it worthwhile investing in new technology development (WDA, 1996b).

At the same time it is clear that since the orientation of the Welsh economy at the end of the twentieth century is towards the so-called 'supply chain' economy, much innovation activity in Welsh companies is directed towards satisfying the needs of the supply chain. However, this is a two-way process and the RTP revealed that innovations and new techniques travel along company supply chains. It was also appar-ent from the RTP that the companies which learn best from each other (WDA, 1996a) were also the most willing to work in industry networks and fora in order to maintain their understanding of the latest techni-ques, technologies and market developments. The Welsh Medical Technology Forum is probably the premier example of such networks (Henderson, 1998), although the Cardiff University Innovation Net-work has also been breaking new ground in the links between academia and industry in the innovation field.

This is important since the RTP underlined that the innovative potential of Wales is hampered by a relatively poor performance in translating academic and research expertise into commercial activity.

Other studies have revealed that the majority of Welsh university interaction with industry is with companies outside Wales, indeed with companies outside the UK (Hill, 1997). A particularly serious weakness in innovation in Wales is that the level of graduate employment in Welsh companies is relatively low. The RTP reasoned that this may be closely related to companies' ability to innovate. During RTP panel discussions, companies observed that their employment of graduates had helped them to carry out innovation projects.

Although, as pointed out earlier in this chapter, there is more to innovation than technology or research and development, the rate at which new 'science' is created is a useful indicator of how much fuel for innovation the economy may hold. Current evidence is not encouraging. Wales appears to have the lowest level of industrial R&D investment of any of the mainland UK regions. Most recent figures show Wales with less than 0.4 per cent of GDP (gross domestic product) being invested by industry in R&D compared to a UK average of some 1.26. (ONS 1998).

The RTP noted that the industrial structure of the Welsh economy may partly account for this. For example, foreign investors do not typically invest in R&D in their operations in Wales, and furthermore, Welsh industry is underrepresented in industry sectors characterised by high research and development investment, for example pharmaceuticals, biotechnology and defence, and Wales does not have any government research establishments which might stimulate private sector concentrations and spin-off benefits in terms of new innovative companies and products. However, there are new grounds for optimism. For example, the implementation of the RTP has placed real investment and new thinking behind the public, academic and private sector enthusiasm for innovation. There has been a refocusing of Objective 2 structural funds and over 60 pilot projects of the RTP have been funded and implemented (WDA, 1998).

At a policy level, the National Assembly published its first National Development Strategy for Wales in July 1999 (NAW, 1999). Innovation and technology were given a new prominence as strategic priorities necessary to contribute to Wales' prosperity. Patient and consistent implementation of appropriate strategies may be among the new Assembly's greatest challenges.

A recent *Innovation Survey* carried out by CBI/NatWest revealed that optimism was greater among Welsh respondents regarding their innovation activities than any other UK region and found, furthermore, that their investment in innovation as a share of turnover was one of the highest reported in the UK (CBI/NatWest, 1999). While subjective measures of optimism have their limitations, and some aspects of the Welsh figures may reflect the influence of publicity given to innovation, any increased awareness within Welsh companies is welcome.

This awareness is a prerequisite for the development of a culture of innovation (WDA, 1996a, 1998). An 'innovative milieu' (Camagni, 1995) is understood to mean much more than investment by firms in new products or processes, or technology transfer from the universities of Wales, but includes also the efforts and attitudes of individuals and society.

Meanwhile, less comfort can be derived from any expectations based on Wales' current economic structure, since the assumption that future strong, innovation-led economic growth will most likely occur in countries or regions where some key sectors have good conditions (Porter, 1990) to innovate and grow does not yet hold for Wales. For example, economies with a high presence of sectors such as biotechnology, information and communications technology (ICT) and environmental technologies can confidently be expected to experience rapid innovation-based, and possibly, sustained growth, while Wales has a poor current representation in such sectors. There is little evidence that this will change in an appropriate timescale, bar small pockets of excellence.

However, economic history is full of examples of new sectors emerging unexpectedly and fortuitously leading to growth in cities, regions and countries, for example the 'Third Italy' (Bagnasco, 1977) and its regions (Cooke and Morgan, 1991). The technologies of the future and the products and businesses that they will bring have probably not been invented yet. Welsh policy-makers and business people must be ready to respond to opportunities as they emerge and, furthermore, create new opportunities where possible. This will require confidence, a willingness to take risks, aspirations to compete with the best, and to reinvestment in the results of successful innovation.

Wales also requires that its institutions are capable of adopting a coherent vision of an innovative society. It will take time, effort and persistence to achieve this goal. The National Assembly should provide the opportunity to create comparative advantage from Wales' 'institutional thickness' (Amin and Thrift, 1994).

Ultimately, the key features necessary to execute the 'shift' are consistent policies and practices of investing in the people of Wales. Wales cannot hope to fully capitalise emergent technology sectors unless it has a prepared, flexible and fully participating workforce, contrary to the mantra repeated by policy-makers and business leaders running the TECs throughout much of the last two decades that 'it is not feasible to invest in training for stock' (see Chapter 3). The information society will require a greater investment in human capital in Wales, by both business and the public sector, than has hitherto been the case. A strategy for raising the value of Wales' human capital and for instilling yet further flexibility and greater innovation must be urgently devised.

Wales in the twenty-first century needs to harness the talents of all its people, not just its scientists and technologists, if it is to rekindle the spirit of innovation ignited during the Industrial Revolution in Wales. Now, as then, an innovative Wales needs to draw upon the innate and educated strengths of its population as well as exploit external sources of ideas and talent.

References

Amin, A. and Thrift, N. (1994) 'Living with the Global', in A. Amin and N. Thrift (eds) *Globalisation, Institutions and Regional Development*, Oxford: Oxford University Press, pp. 1–22.

Bagnasco, A. (1977) *Tre Italie. La Problematica Territoriale dello Sviluppo Italiano*, Bologna: Il Mulino.

Camagni, R. (1995) 'The Concept of the Innovative Milieu and its Relevance for Public Policies in Lagging Regions', *Papers in Regional Science*, vol. 74(4), pp. 317–40.

Collins (1997) *Collins Concise Dictionary*, Glasgow: HarperCollins.

Confederation of Business and Industry/Natl West (1999) *Innovation Survey*, London: CBI.

Cooke, P.N. and Morgan, K. (1998) *The Associational Economy. Firms, Regions and Innovation*, Oxford: Oxford University Press.

Cooke, P.N. and Morgan, K. (1991) 'The Intelligent Region: Industrial and Institutional Innovation in Emilia-Romagna', Regional Industrial Research Report no. 7, Cardiff: University of Wales.

Cooke, P.N. and Morgan, K. (1990) 'Learning through Networking: Regional Innovation and the Lessons of Baden Wurttemberg', Regional Industrial Research Report no. 5, Cardiff: University of Wales.

Department of Trade and Industry (1998) White Paper, *Our Competitive Future: Building the Knowledge Driven Economy*, London: HMSO, Cm 4176.

European Commission (1995) Green Paper on *Innovation*, COM (95) 688.

European Commission (1996) *First Action Plan for Innovation in Europe*, COM (96) 589 final.

Funk, J.L. (1992) *The Teamwork Advantage: An Inside Look at Japanese Product and Technology Development*, Cambridge, Mass.: Productivity Press.

Henderson, D. (1998) 'Building Interactive Learning Networks: Lessons from the Welsh Medical Technological Forum', *Regional Studies*, vol. 32 (8), pp. 783–7.

Hill, S. *et al.* (1997) 'The Impact of the Higher Education Sector in the Welsh Economy: Measurement, Analysis and Enhancement', University of Wales, April 1997.

Morgan, K. and Nauwelaers, C. (eds) (1999) *Regional Innovation Strategies: The Challenge for Less Favoured Regions*, London: Jessica Kingsley.

Morgan, K.O. (1981) *Rebirth of a Nation. Wales 1880–1980,* Oxford: Clarendon Press.

National Assembly for Wales (1999) *National Economic Strategy for Wales*, consultative document, Cardiff: NAW.

ONS (1998) *Regional Trends* London: HMSO.

Porter, M. (1990) *The Competitive Advantage of Nations*, New York: Free Press.

Welsh Development Agency (1996a) *Wales Regional Technology Plan. An Innovation and Technology Strategy for Wales. Action Plan*, Cardiff: WDA.

Welsh Development Agency (1996b) *Wales Regional Technology Plan: An Innovation and Technology Strategy for Wales. Consultation Paper*, Cardiff: WDA.

Welsh Development Agency (1998) *Wales Regional Technology Plan: An Innovation and Technology Strategy for Wales. Review and Update*, Cardiff: WDA.

Williams, G.A. (1985) *When Was Wales?*, Harmondsworth: Penguin.

10 Setting Policy Targets and Evaluating Performance

Annette Roberts

INTRODUCTION

The purpose of this book has been to review past Welsh economic performance, and to suggest and comment on policy alternatives to improve Wales' future economic position, in terms of general prosperity. This will be achieved by enhancing the scope and depth of economic activity in the next century

Preceding chapters have hinted at gaps in available information, and there have been many arguments for research to further understanding of the ways in which the economy works. There has been commentary on the problems of the Welsh economy, along with discussion of possible solutions. However, information to assist the decision-making process in choosing between alternative policies is sparse, and methodologies are needed for a rigorous evaluation of the efficacy of current and potential future policies. These are complex empirical issues, not least because of the difficulties in disentangling policy impact from what would have happened in the absence of policy action. These are increasingly important matters, particularly in Scotland and Wales where newly-devolved governments are hungry for information and where transparency in policy-making will be demanded as well as clear evidence of success or failure.

> Objectives have to be underpinned by clear targets and indicators against which everyone can measure progress. There needs to be a clear hierarchy of targets and associated indicators, linking directly to the strategic objectives and feeding through to European and domestic programme activity. (European Task Force, 1999, p. 12)

This chapter seeks to provide a review of the issues, problems and potentials for policy evaluation in Wales. The first section will briefly review earlier chapters, drawing together policy options whilst also providing comment on targets set for the Welsh economy over the next decade. We then consider measurement and evaluation approaches at the regional level; such approaches should aid understanding about the effectiveness of policy, allow alternatives to be assessed, and enable Welsh economic performance to be compared to other regions or countries with a view to ultimately guiding resource-allocation decisions. The concluding section outlines possible future outcomes.

OPTIONS AND TARGETS

The Welsh economic problem has been defined and summarised in terms of a poor GDP per capita performance relative to the UK and EU average (WDA, 1999a). Earlier chapters have analysed the underlying causes of this poor economic performance. Industrial structure and occupational mix resulting in low wages, low participation rates, underperformance of the SME sector, and difficulties in the rural economy have all contributed. Each of these, and other issues, have been discussed alongside a set of possible scenarios for improvement, whilst a more local analysis of the possibilities arising out of EU Objective 1 funding for west Wales and the valleys has also been set out.

The policy options emerging as a result include encouraging higher value-added employment, skills development and providing aid to small firms. However, there is at present no framework to enable the impact of policies to be fully assessed and monitored. Throughout this book there has also been a focus on the need for realistic policies and targets, and for ensuring that alternatives are consistent with one another. Of critical importance is the issue of opportunity cost in economic policy decisions; with limited resources, policy choice inevitably means forgoing alternatives in spite of the possibilities for complementary approaches.

The consultation document *Proposals for a National Economic Development Strategy* published by the European Task Force in July 1999, includes 'strategic targets', setting time limits for relative GDP improvement. For example, at an all-Wales level, per capita GDP was targeted to reach 84 per cent of the UK average by 2002, 87 per cent of the UK average by 2006, and 90 per cent of the UK average by 2010. Per capita GDP in west Wales and the valleys was targeted to reach 75 per cent of the UK average by 2002, 78 per cent by 2006, and 81 per cent by 2010.

The implications of the target of Welsh GDP per capita equalling 90 per cent of UK levels are set out in an earlier WDA consultation document (WDA, 1999a). This target would require Welsh GDP growth to average over 4 per cent per annum for the next 10 years. In contrast, over the last 10 years Welsh real GDP has grown by less than 1 per cent per annum (Cambridge Econometrics, 1999). Earlier years had seen higher growth rates, for example during the consumer boom of the mid–late 1980s, which were not sustainable. However, if Wales is to close the GDP differential with the rest of the UK then by definition it must consistently achieve higher growth rates than the UK. In addition, if the poorest parts of Wales are to improve their economic performance relative to the rest of Wales they need to grow even faster. Even apparently modest targets represent a substantial challenge for policy-makers in Wales. For example, the European Task Force consultation document mentioned above also contained 'associated targets', such as net additional jobs in Wales to increase by 40 000 by 2002, by a further 48 000 by 2006, and by a further 48 000 by 2010. Hence, the 2010 target total anticipates almost 140 000 net additional jobs. Assuming that the target is for gross jobs, with full-time and part-time given equal weighting and that self-employment is included, then over an 11-year period this implies an annual growth rate of just over 1 per cent in Welsh employment. This compares to a projected employment growth rate of 0.5 per cent per annum (Cambridge Econometrics, 1999). If this target is to be consistent with the GDP target, the jobs must be full-time high value-added jobs. However, the changing industrial structure and the growth of service sector employment has been accompanied by a decline in this type of employment in more recent years (see Chapters 2 and 3). The 'intermediate targets' for skills, innovation and added value will then be crucial to the achievement of these job targets.

Whatever target levels are agreed by policy-makers in Wales, they should be challenging, but realistic and consistent. Effective policy evaluation and monitoring will also require clear technical guidelines, for example about how jobs are counted, and what weight should be given to part-time and temporary work.

A further consideration is the National Assembly's commitment to 'sustainability'. As Bristow (Chapter 6) illustrates, sustainability issues will have a major influence on Assembly policy. This commitment appears to be far greater than in other regions of the UK, and may then act as a brake on economic growth to a greater extent than for competitor regions, whether this be through conflict over transport infrastructure, through the selective attraction of relatively non-polluting industries, or through greater emphasis on potentially costly sustainable methods. It is as yet too early to assess whether such a commitment will be a hindrance to economic growth, or whether Wales can develop a comparative advantage in new 'green' industries.

GDP, employment and productivity gaps relate Wales to the rest of UK, and this chapter has already demonstrated some of the challenges of reducing these gaps. However, Wales' economic position within the EU and the global economy could be usefully established. For example, the north-east England *Competitiveness Project* benchmarked the north-east region against comparator regions (similar in size, GDP, employment and so on), exemplar regions (for example Four Motor regions, as well as the south-east of England) and competitors for inward investment (Charles and Benneworth, 1996). Chapter 4 has already discussed the threat to future FDI in Wales from UK and EU regions. An analysis of Wales' performance in terms of comparators, perhaps those outside the UK, may be as valuable as relating targets to UK or EU averages.

EVALUATION APPROACHES

Policy evaluation in Wales has typically followed an accounting or value for money approach, whereby, for example, the number of jobs created or safeguarded are measured and then offset against grant-aid costs. This methodology has been applied in evaluations of Regional Selective Assistance (RSA – discretionary grant aid paid to companies in Assisted Areas) in Wales and elsewhere (see Munday *et al.*, 1999 for a review of RSA in Wales). However, these narrow evaluation approaches are partly a consequence of the equally narrow policy objectives which have tended to be defined simply in terms of job-creation. These methodologies have the principal concern of measuring value for (public) money, to decide, generally after the event, whether grant aid has been well-spent. Wider objectives, encompassing the economywide impacts of policy, should lead to broader evaluation frameworks where impacts and opportunity costs can be fully assessed. In addition, policy 'risks' may be necessary to achieve a turnaround in Welsh economic fortunes. Accountability frameworks would then need to provide some flexibility for more creative policy-making.

Alternatives that extend the accounting approach have been proposed. For example, Swales (1997) developed a cost–benefit methodology for RSA evaluation, using shadow prices, to estimate the level of grant aid that would make a particular project fiscally neutral (where the grant aid and associated costs are fully offset by tax payments resulting from new jobs and so on). Other extensions include the various economic modelling approaches to evaluation and impact assessment. In each case, reliable quantitative data is required as an input; different outputs and consequences can then be assessed.

A recent WDA working paper (Roberts *et al.*, 1999) provided an overview of recent and potential methodological developments in policy-evaluation. A number of different approaches to modelling the Welsh economy already exist, using a range of data sources and methods. Models of the Welsh economy have been developed by academics, and by national forecasting organisations such as Cambridge Econometrics (CE), Business Strategies Limited (BSL), and Northern Ireland Economic Research Centre (NIERC) – see Bell (1993) for a review of CE and NIERC approaches. These modelling approaches are, however, unable to systematically capture the full impacts of policies. These difficulties are compounded at the small-area level because data is unavailable, or time lags of several years apply. Sample sizes are often small, reducing the reliability of information (Higgs *et al.*, 1999).

The impact of economic change and policy has been assessed using *Welsh Input–Output Tables*. These tables provide a detailed financial account of the trading relationships between industries within and outside Wales, and by further manipulation allow the knock-on or multiplier impacts of projects to be estimated (see Brand *et al.*, 1998 for a description of the methodology and data sources). These tables have been used to compare the potential impacts of alternative inward investment policies (Hill and Roberts, 1998), to explore the impacts of infrastructure improvements (Bryan *et al.*, 1997), and to estimate the significance of particular industries or sectors (Bryan *et al.*, 1998).

Whilst this methodology provides a useful framework, it has limitations. The demand-driven modelling approach is useful for estimating the quantitative impact of particular policies only where the direct output or employment changes as a result can be quantified and incorporated into the framework. For example, the potential GDP impact of an export-promotion strategy can be estimated using this methodology – various scenarios can be explored. According to *Welsh I–O Table* estimates, a 10 per cent increase in overseas exports from Wales would increase Welsh GDP by around 1.5 per cent.

However, the many development policies that aim to generate supply-side improvements are much more difficult to estimate systematically, other than by assumption. For example, skills development is a key policy issue in Wales. The *Future Skills Wales* report (MORI/BSL, 1999) provided detailed survey-derived information on prospective employee needs and individual aspirations. However, generating quantitative estimates of the likely impacts of a skills-development policy is extremely complex. Individuals in Wales have different labour-market characteristics and hence receive differential pay rates compared to the rest of the UK (Blackaby *et al.*, 1999). If, for example, Welsh educational achievements matched the UK average, then, according to these estimates, earnings in Wales would be 1 per cent higher. However, more importantly, individuals in Wales receive lower economic 'rewards' (pay) for the same labour market characteristics compared to the rest of the UK (due to other factors such as lack of effective demand).

If the overall level of skills in Wales were to increase, what would be the impact? This depends on a mix of supply and demand factors, and on the sectoral distribution of impacts. The employment, output and GDP impacts of such policies are not easy to predict, and more research is needed. Possibilities for future modelling and evaluation frameworks in Wales are still being explored, and include combining methodologies to integrate demand and supply, and supplementing existing frameworks with more qualitative research or case-study information on policy impacts.

FUTURE DEVELOPMENTS

The next century will see ever-increasing demand for information on small-area economies and policy impacts. Regional development agencies (RDAs) are becoming accountable, and will require better information systems for resource allocation, rather than for post-policy evaluation. For example, the WDA has recognised the need for more data and has made a commitment to the improved measurement of its own performance, concentrating on impact rather than activity (WDA, 1999b, p. 15).

One consequence of these information requirements at a regional and sub-regional level must be improvements in data availability and reliability, which will help to provide a better understanding of how our local economies work, with improved evaluation methods leading to more effective resource allocation. None of this can be achieved instantly. For the short term, priorities need to be established, with realistic options and targets, recognising that choosing one particular option inevitably means giving up something else in return. For the longer term, RDAs need a performance-monitoring framework that allows policy decisions to be more finely tuned towards defined objectives.

References

Bell, N.F. (1993) 'Regional Econometric Modelling in the UK: A Review', *Regional Studies*, 27(8), pp. 777–82.

Blackaby, D., Murphy, P. and O'Leary, N. (1999) *Income, Earnings and Prices*, Cardiff: WDA.

Brand, S., Hill, S. and Roberts, A. (1998) *Welsh Input–Output Tables for 1995*, Cardiff: University of Wales Press.

Bryan, J., Clarke, D., Hill, S., Munday, M. and Roberts, A. (1998) 'The Economic Impact of the Arts and Cultural Industries in Wales', WERU, 43 Park Place, Cardiff, CF13BB.

Cambridge Econometrics (1999) *Regional Economic Prospects*, Cambridge: CE.

Charles, D. and Benneworth, P. (1996) *The Competitiveness Project*, Centre for Urban and Regional Development Studies, Newcastle University.

European Task Force (1999) *Proposals for a National Economic Development Strategy, A Consultation Document*, Cardiff: National Assembly of Wales, July.

Higgs, G., Hill, S., Roberts, A. and White, S. (1999) *Economic and Social Indicators for Wales*, Newtown: Mid Wales Partnership.

Hill, S. and Roberts, A. (1998) 'Inward Investment, Local Linkages and Regional Development', in S. Hill and B. Morgan (eds), *Inward Investment, Business Finance and Regional Development*, London: Macmillan.

Hill, S., McNicoll, I. and Roberts, A. (1999) 'The Economic Effectiveness of Higher Education in "Nation" Regions of the UK: A Comparative Study of Scotland and Wales', *Higher Education Management*, vol. II no.3 pp. 127–42.

MORI/BSL Ltd (1999) *Future Skills Wales: Main Report* (available from any Welsh Training and Enterprise Council).

Munday, M., Pickernell, P. and Roberts, A. (1999) 'The Effectiveness of Regional Grant Aid: A Welsh Perspective', paper presented at the Regional Science Association European Congress, Dublin, August.

Roberts, A., Jones, C. and Taylor, K. (1999) *Measuring the Impact of Development Policy: Methodological Issues and Potential Solutions*, working paper, Cardiff: WDA.

Swales, J.K. (1997) 'A Cost–Benefit Approach to the Evaluation of Regional Selective Assistance', *Fiscal Studies*, vol. 18 (1), February, pp. 73–85.

Welsh Development Agency (1999a) *Towards an Economic Analysis of Wales, Consultation Document*, Cardiff: WDA, May.

Welsh Development Agency (1999b) *Promoting Prosperity, WDA Corporate Plan 2000–2003, Consultation Document*, Cardiff: WDA: July.

Bryan, J., Hill, S., Munday, M. and Roberts, A. (1997), 'Road Infrastructure and Economic Development in the Periphery: The Case of the A55 Improvements in North Wales', *Journal of Transport Geography*, vol. 5, no. 4, pp. 227–37.

11 Shaping the Future

Stephen Hill

INTRODUCTION

The interested reader, having worked through an eclectic combination of chapters of diverse style, approaches and opinions, could appropriately be considering the one question most feared by academics – so what? Recognising that knowledge and understanding are intrinsically important is one thing – wading through pages of detail mixed with polemic is quite another. This relatively short chapter will seek to identify threads from the previous chapters, and weave them together with a great deal of personal opinion in order to set out some possible solutions to the fundamental challenge that has dominated this book: how to engender the kind of shift in growth that will, in the medium term, place the typical citizen in Wales on a par in terms of living standards with their UK counterparts. That such an achievement has eluded Wales in the last century does not make this an unachievable task, but it does underline the seriousness of the challenge.

GROWTH TARGETS AND THEIR IMPLICATIONS

Some simple arithmetic also emphasises the scale of that challenge. Assume (since the figures are not yet available), that Welsh GDP per head in the year 2000 was 82 per cent of the UK average, and that the economic development target was for Welsh GDP/head to reach 90 per cent of the UK average by 2010 (as in the *National Economic Development Strategy*, European Task Force, 1999), and be on a par with the UK by 2025. How fast the Welsh economy then has to grow to catch up depends on the growth rate of the UK economy. Table 11.1 sets out Welsh and UK GDP growth rates in real terms, both over the past three decades and as anticipated over the next decade by Cambridge Econometrics (1999).

Taking the prediction that the UK economy will grow in real terms by 2.7 per cent per annum over the next decade, and then extrapolating beyond the next decade, provides the basis for the simple calculations of Table 11.2.

Table 11.1   Annual real percentage change in GDP

	1971–80	1980–90	1990–95	1995–00	2000–05	2005–10
Wales	1.5	2.9	1.2	1.7	2.3	2.5
UK	1.5	2.7	1.5	2.2	2.7	2.7

Source: Cambridge Econometrics (1999).

Table 11.2   Achieving targets for Wales

Year	UK GDP/head	Wales as % of UK	Wales/UK	Implied growth
2000	100	82	82	
2010	130.5	90	117.5	3.7
2025	194.7	110	194.7	3.4

The first data column of Table 11.2 sets UK GDP/head at 100 and then calculates UK GDP/head in 2010 and 2025, assuming a real growth rate of 2.7 per cent per annum. By 2025, UK GDP/head will have almost doubled in real terms if the Cambridge Econometrics forecast is correct. The next column then assumes Welsh GDP/head as 82 per cent of the UK level in 2000, rising to 90 per cent by 2010 and to parity by 2025. Then, relative to the UK GDP/head indexed to 100 in the year 2000, Welsh GDP/head must rise to 117.5 by 2010, an annual growth rate averaging 3.7 per cent per annum until then, and by 3.4 per cent afterwards to 2025. Hence, in the decade to 2010, Welsh GDP must grow by at least 1 per cent per annum faster than the UK to reach the 90 per cent target, and by rather more than this in later years if the shorter term forecasts in Table 11.1 are correct.

One approach to this challenge, and a fairly sensible one, is to ask the question of what kind of policy achievements would be necessary to raise the GDP growth rate in Wales by a particular amount. Alternately and equivalently, what impact would be necessary in order to lift the Welsh growth rates anticipated in Table 11.1 to those required by Table 11.2, if the relative targets are to be met. In other words, what impacts would increase Welsh GDP by (say) 1 per cent, noting that this would have to be additional to the growth already forecast in Table 11.1.

The methodological problem is then that of assessing the likely impact of policy implementation on Welsh GDP. The previous chapters have amply demonstrated that the prosperity gap is the result of both not having enough people in work (*the activity rate gap*) and not generating enough income (or GDP) from the ones that are working, (*the productivity gap*). Hence, raising the Welsh GDP growth rate must be about generating more jobs (self-employed as well as employed) as well as making those jobs more productive, most especially by a shift into fast growing and value-adding tradable services. There are a wide range of possible policies and initiatives for engendering these kinds of shifts, all the way from the blanket provision of communications technology in schools and colleges, through to the retraining (and remotivating) of older workers. However, the analysis of this book has made it abundantly clear that supply-side measures such as these will not, on their own, be sufficient to stimulate the level of growth needed and must be matched by demand stimulation; that is, the generation of substantially more trade for businesses in Wales.

Estimates of the level of demand stimulus necessary to achieve a 1 percentage point shift in the Welsh growth rate are set out in Table 11.3, derived by manipulation of the 1996 *Welsh Input–Output Tables* (Hill and Roberts, 2000). These input–output tables, the product of a continuing research project at the Welsh Economy Research Unit of Cardiff Business School, quantify the detailed relationships between the many sectors in the Welsh economy, as well as purchases and sales between Welsh firms, the rest of the UK and overseas. The impact of a change in one part of an economy will ripple across that economy according to the trading relationships between the various sectors that make up the economy. Table 11.3 suggests that a 1 per cent increase in Welsh GDP could be achieved by a 6.8 per cent increase in overseas exports from Wales, by a 1.9 per cent increase in exports to the rest of UK and overseas or by a more general 0.7 per cent increase in gross output (or turnover) in Wales. Each of these would generate between 8000 and 10 000 full-time equivalent jobs.

Other alternatives that could be modelled include a change in the output of a particular sector or sectors, including the attraction of new manufacturing investment such as the Sony complex at Bridgend. For

Table 11.3 Changes to increase Welsh GDP by 1 per cent

	%	*Increase in jobs*
Increase overseas exports by:	6.8	8610
Increase rest of UK and overseas exports by:	1.9	8970
Increase gross output (turnover) by:	0.7	9530

example a 30 per cent increase in output by the Electronics sector in Wales would be necessary to increase Welsh GDP by 1 per cent. However, the lesson from this kind of sectoral analysis is that the burden of required change is simply too great for individual sectors or projects. The best medium term prospects for achieving the targets lie within export promotion, allied to a longer term investment strategy around the likely requirements of a competitive region in the global twenty-first century economy.

Table 11.3, however, can say nothing about the kind of policies necessary to achieve those changes or their relative cost-effectiveness. Moreover, use of the modelling framework carries the implicit risk of only concentrating on those activities or programmes for which the direct impacts can be quantified. Issues such as changing attitudes and culture may be equally effective but are much harder to evaluate.

NEW THINKING

As noted in Chapter 1, regional economies are evolving in a process of continuous change that may accelerate or decelerate at various times, but which always defies expectations. One consequence of rapid change is that notions of the economy can get seriously out of step with reality. This book should have expelled rather than reinforced some of these misperceptions, hopefully by presenting the Welsh economy as it is rather than by replacing one set of misconceptions with another. This section will be explicit about some current misconceptions, the final section will set out the likely characteristics of successful and prosperous regional economies in the new century, and will argue for a much broader scope to the economic development effort in Wales.

Old Notions

1. *Economic development policy as politically driven, responding to short-term needs on the implicit assumption that long-term growth will follow.* This is a familiar, if dangerous notion, with its major consequence being an apparently endless stream of initiatives and 'pilots', some of which have been very effective but none of which have been continued on a sufficient scale or time period to seriously impact on the prosperity gap. Examples include recurrent and apparently successful but short-lived attempts to foster enterprise in schools and small-scale venture capital initiatives. It is here that

the National Assembly can have greatest impact, either positive or negative. A visionary Assembly will recognise the need for long-term investment and will encourage the development of enterprise inside a risk-assessing rather than risk-minimising framework. A parochial or short-sighted Assembly will demand instant results that immediately reach all corners of Wales and its economy – and hence paralyse long-term growth. A far-sighted Assembly might rather consider, for example, sacrificing current consumption for long-term gain as in investing on a radical scale in marketing skills, including the maximum application of e-commerce through both technology infrastructure and appropriate training.

2. *The Welsh economy is dominated by large, foreign-owned manufacturers.* Examples of this misconception can be found in the manifestos of the political parties for the first Assembly elections, and in the deliberations of the Welsh Affairs Committee. The consequence of this notion is that large foreign-owned manufacturers can then be blamed for the failure to close the prosperity gap. In fact, as the observant reader will have noted, whilst manufacturing is certainly relatively more important to Wales than the UK average, manufacturing itself provides just over a fifth of employment in Wales (but rather more in terms of GDP). Moreover, foreign-owned manufacturing is just a small proportion of this, providing in total some 70 000 jobs or about 6 per cent of the Welsh workforce. Indeed, public services employ roughly four times as many people in Wales as do overseas manufacturers.

More importantly in a global economy, the very notion of 'foreignness' is becoming outmoded. Not only do current figures underestimate the extent of multinational involvement in any regional economy, since they ignore the (presumably) high level of British-owned multinational activity, but also the concept of attaching national ownership to global enterprise is increasingly irrelevant. For example, current figures for foreign direct investment in Wales include companies that have been operating in Wales for half a century or more, whilst even 'indigenous' companies like British Steel operate in many countries and are owned in part by shareholders far beyond British shores.

In terms of economic development it may make little differences whether operations in Wales are controlled from London, Seoul or New York. The point is that Wales must compete in a global economy, and will prosper or otherwise according to how well it can create the conditions that encourage enterprises to develop and grow. This does not imply that help should not be given to new companies and existing small firms – rather, that the origins of the enterprise are much less important than its effects. Foreign investment has brought jobs, high productivity and GDP to Wales.

3. *Social development is more important than economic development in Wales.* There is no doubt that there are serious inequalities within Wales, with more prosperous parts of south-east and north-east Wales offset by poorer areas, particularly in west Wales and the valleys, and that there are severe social consequences of this. However, these social consequences are themselves the product of persistent low incomes reflected in the GDP gap: enduring poverty robs communities of ambition and motivation, as well as their most able people. A Wales with prosperity 18 per cent below the UK average must concentrate on economic growth, which can and should be complementary to social development, nurturing and encouraging local communities to maximise their own contribution to well-being.

NEW CHALLENGES

Given the dominant challenge of closing the prosperity gap between Wales and the UK average, a long-term vision for Wales must identify the likely characteristics of a prosperous region in a UK (and EU) context, and then outline the steps necessary in the process of change towards that vision.

A prosperous Wales in the new century is likely to possess ample quantities of the following qualities:

- High levels of value-added in products and process;
- Some resources devoted to generating new knowledge, but many more to the dissemination and application of existing knowledge;
- An attractive physical and business environment for the (relatively few) creative and enterprising people who will drive economic growth;
- A Wales-wide network of information and communications infrastructure that allows outward-looking individuals and companies to trade globally;
- Appropriate social capital (values, culture and key institutions) to deliver cohesion and growth;

- Vibrant creative industries, generating and delivering content in a wide variety of forms; and
- Physical infrastructure that carries development and growth across Wales, allowing all communities to participate in the economic growth process.

An optimist would see the seeds of some of these characteristics in current Wales, pointing to the *National Economic Development Strategy* as bringing together the public and private sectors inside a framework that both raises growth aspirations and seeks delivery mechanisms to achieve them. Other strengths include the growing confidence of policy-makers in the new institutional arrangements in Wales, and a determination to make these work. Whilst control over the macro-economic environment may remain in Whitehall, responsibility for the state of the Welsh economy has shifted to the National Assembly in Cardiff, including the all-important imperative of creating the appropriate business environment for growth.

The same optimist would point also to the rapidly-emerging creative industries in Wales, with Cardiff leading the way in developing informal networks of individuals and organisations that are giving credibility to the notion of a knowledge-based economy, with increasing connections between media, arts and theatre performance, software and design, and a variety of associated professional services. At the same time Wales retains traditional strengths in manufacturing, with high levels of earnings, productivity and external trade providing a firm foundation for the continuing shift towards value-adding services.

At the opposite end of the spectrum, a pessimist would see the continuing importance of manufacturing as binding the Welsh economy to a slow-growth future, given the global shift towards tradable services. Similarly the age of devolution could provide new scope for parochialism and introspection, fed by the apparently studied indifference of a large proportion of the Welsh people as evidenced by the low turnout in the first Assembly elections in 1999.

This, of course, brings this book, full circle, back to the starting point in Chapter 1: *There are indeed many ways of looking at the world . . .*

References

Cambridge Econometrics (1999) *Regional Economic Prospects: Analysis and Forecasts to 2010*, Cambridge, July.

European Task Force (1999) *Proposals for a National Economic Development Strategy, A Consultation Document*, July, Cardiff: National Assembly of Wales.

Hill, S. and Roberts, A. (2000) *Welsh Input–Output Table for 1996*, Cardiff: University of Wales Press.

Index